THE RELUCTANT PROPHET
Jonah Through New Eyes

Uri Brito
and Rich Lusk

WEST MONROE, LOUISIANA

The Reluctant Prophet: Jonah Through New Eyes
By Uri Brito & Rich Lusk
Copyright © 2021 by Athanasius Press
715 Cypress Street
West Monroe, Louisiana 71291
www.athanasiuspress.org

ISBN: 978-1-7351690-7-1 (softcover)

All rights reserved. No part of this publication may be reproduced, stored in a retrieval system, or transmitted in any form or by any means—electronic, mechanical, photocopy, recording, or any other—except for brief quotations in printed reviews, without the prior permission of the publisher.

This publication contains The Holy Bible, English Standard Version®, copyright © 2001 by Crossway Bibles, a publishing ministry of Good News Publishers. The ESV® text appearing in this publication is reproduced and published by cooperation between Good News Publishers and Athanasius Press and by permission of Good News Publishers. Unauthorized reproduction of this publication is prohibited.

The Holy Bible, English Standard Version (ESV) is adapted from the Revised Standard Version of the Bible, copyright Division of Christian Education of the National Council of the Churches of Christ in the U.S.A. All rights reserved.

English Standard Version®, ESV®, and the ESV® logo are trademarks of Good News Publishers located in Wheaton, Illinois. Used by permission.

Contents

	Introduction	v
1	Repentance Unto Life	1
2	The Psalm of Jonah	13
3	Nineveh Overturned	35
4	Jonah's Last Stand	53
	Appendix A: Biography of Human Maturation	73
	Appendix B: Does God Change His Mind?	81
	Appendix C: Jonah and the Missional Church	97

Introduction

Matthew 12:38-42 & Jonah 1-4

Why would Jesus compare Himself to a disobedient prophet like Jonah, as He does in Matthew 12:41 when He identifies Himself as the One "greater than Jonah"? Why was it significant for Jesus to refer to Jonah in the first place? Unlike Jonah, Jesus did not rebel against His calling. Jesus is unmistakably greater than Jonah! Given how he bucked God's commands, we might even say Jonah was the least of all the prophets. There were many prophets who were greater than Jonah—not just Jesus.

When Jesus declares Himself to be "greater than Jonah," He is referring not only to the man Jonah with all his shortcomings but also to the whole story of which Jonah is a part. Jesus presents Himself as the fulfillment of the typological pattern manifested in the narrative of Jonah. In this sense, Jonah is a type of the Lord Jesus Christ, even in spite of himself. The dynamics at work in Jonah's generation are a foreshadowing of things to come at the beginning of the Gospel era—in Jesus' generation. Jonah, unwittingly, points away from himself to Jesus, and his generation points ahead to the generation of Jesus' day.

To understand what Jesus is getting at when He says that He is greater than Jonah, we must look at the book of Jonah as a whole. Indeed, the Jonah story is historical; the events happened just as the book records. But it is also a symbolic story, prophetic of Israel's future. Therefore, Jonah can serve as a sign. The book must be read as a narrative that signifies something beyond the historical facts it records.

THE MULTILAYERED TYPOLOGY OF JONAH[1]

How should we understand the typology of the Book of Jonah? Before we can understand how Jonah serves as a type of Christ, we must see how he was a type, or representative, of Israel. We move from Jonah to Israel, then from Israel to Jesus, and then finally from Jesus to the Church. This series of allusions may not be the way we are accustomed to reading the Scriptures, but it is undoubtedly the way Jesus and the Apostles read their Old Testament. If all these interrelationships and layers of meaning do not become immediately evident in this chapter, perhaps they will be more apparent by the end of our commentary.

As we turn to the story of Jonah, there are at least two items that strike us as odd. First, the word of the Lord comes to Jonah, but it sends him not to Israel's king, as is usually the case throughout the Old Testament, but instead to a Gentile city, Nineveh, the capital of the Assyrian empire (1:1-2). Jonah is called to minister "out of bounds" in a non-Jewish region. He is called away from his local parish ministry to a short-term foreign mission trip.

Second, and even more shocking, Jonah disobeys this calling. He runs the other way (1:3). Now, for a prophet to reluctantly accept his calling is not that unusual in the Old Testament. We

---

1   Our understanding of typology in general and of the typology of Jonah is heavily dependent on the various works of Peter J. Leithart, including his sermon on "The Sign of Jonah," preached at Christ Church, Moscow, ID. Additionally, see James B. Jordan's lectures delivered at Providence Church in Pensacola, Fl.

might think of Moses, who was not exactly enthusiastic about going before Pharaoh, or of Jeremiah, who also was hesitant to take up the prophet's mantle. But Jonah's case is much more extreme. Jonah disobeys from the outset. God says to go this way, and Jonah goes that way. Jonah would rather cease being a prophet than go to Nineveh.

Jonah's disobedience raises an important point we will return to again and again in this study because it is so critical to understanding this book. We must ask, why did Jonah resist going to Nineveh? What motivated him to disobey? Some say Jonah must have been a coward, but we do not believe that is the answer. Instead, we affirm that Jonah knows what this assignment meant for his work. He knows that Israel is in danger of exile because of her sin (Lev. 26; Deut. 28), and he knows that Assyria can serve as the instrument through which God will judge Israel and drive her into exile. Indeed, Assyria was already encroaching on territory close to Israel. Jonah knows that if God sends him to preach in Nineveh, God must have merciful intentions toward the Ninevites since God's offer of grace always accompanies His Word. Otherwise, God would simply judge the pagan city without warning, as He did with many other Gentile nations.

Jonah, perhaps because of his prophetic training, sees the big picture. He knows that Israel deserves punishment under the terms of the covenant laid out in Leviticus and Deuteronomy. The prophet knows that Assyria is the rising world empire and thus the prime candidate to bring the judgment, so he puts two and two together. His thinking would have gone something like this: If God sends me to preach to the Ninevites, He must intend mercy toward them. If I preach to the Ninevites, they will repent, and if they repent, they will become a stronger empire. And if the Ninevites get stronger, they will conquer unrepentant Israel for sure (cf. Jonah 4:2). Jonah wants to play no part in helping an enemy nation conquer his own. He does not wish to be considered a traitor by his own people.

We assert that this is the ultimate source of Jonah's sin. He is not a coward; instead, he is a patriot. Typically, patriotism is a virtue. After all, the love of nation is simply an extension of love for family. But these loves can become disordered; we can love a good thing wrongly or to an unhealthy extent. Jonah has become so patriotic that he has become an idolater. Jonah loves Israel more than he loves God. Or we could say Jonah hates Ninevah more than he loves God. Jonah is committed to Israel, whether she is right or wrong. He is determined to protect himself and his own nation, even at the cost of disobedience. He understands the divine promise underlying his call to Nineveh: If the word is going from Israel to the Gentiles, it is a sign that Israel will be judged and rejected; it is a sign that God desires to provoke Israel to jealousy, and Jonah wants no part of it.

Jonah would have gleaned all this from familiar passages like the Song of Moses in Deuteronomy 32, a hymn Jonah probably grew up singing. The text gives something of a *lex talionis* pattern: eye for eye, tooth for tooth, jealousy for jealousy. In the Song of Moses, God tells Israel that if she provokes Him to jealousy by worshiping idols, Yahweh will provoke Israel to jealousy by giving Himself to the Gentiles. Israel has gone after other gods so God will turn His attention to other nations.

Jonah's Failed Escape

Jonah disobeys the command to preach in Ninevah by fleeing in the opposite direction. Jonah's flight is one filled with ironies. When the sailors finally wake him up, he confesses that his God made the sea and the dry land (1:9). Considering this theologically proper confession, we may be prompted to inquire: If your God is the Creator and sovereign over the sea, why are you trying to flee from Him by way of the sea? Indeed there is no escape from the presence of the Lord.

Moreover, Jonah is fleeing so that he will not have to preach to Gentiles. He does not want to help convert Gentiles to the worship of Israel's God. And yet on the ship, he says one sentence to these Gentile sailors, and they all convert on the spot. They begin to call on Yahweh and offer sacrifice (1:10-16). Of course, this is a foreshadowing of what is going to happen when Jonah goes to Nineveh. He cannot escape his prophetic calling. The word of the Lord will be effectual even if it is preached in spite of Jonah's heart.

There also is a contrast between these Gentile sailors and Israel. God sent prophet after prophet after prophet to Israel. And still, Israel showed no sign of repentance. But these Gentiles get one prophet who utters one sentence of biblical testimony (1:9) and immediately fall on their faces in repentance. The roles reverse themselves. The Gentiles model a proper response to God's word.

Unlike the impressionable, receptive sailors, Jonah refuses to repent, even in the face of the disastrous storm. His sin endangers the lives of these Gentile sailors, but he is calloused. He is a picture of Israel's condition at that time. Jonah's actions are not altruistic but egoistic.

If he had repented, Jonah would have demanded the crew turn the boat around to Nineveh, but he would rather die than go to Nineveh. And so, he says, "Throw me into the sea! Cast me overboard to calm the storm!" The sailors reluctantly do so, begging that God will be merciful to them because they do not intend to shed innocent blood. Their piety stands in stark contrast with Jonah's willful and self-centered rebellion.

The Lord has a plan through all of this, of course. Jonah is thrown overboard, but the Lord preserves Jonah in a great fish (1:17). Here again, it is significant to grasp the bigger biblical picture to grasp the unfolding story. Prophets would frequently not only tell of coming judgments upon Israel but act out those judgments. They would not only foretell what was to come, but they would dramatize their message. They would engage in symbolic, prophetic actions. We might think of Isaiah dressing up as a slave to show what will happen to Israel in exile, or Jeremiah, who had a clay pot made and then crushed it before the eyes of the Israelites to show what would happen to them when judgment fell. Or we might think of Jesus as a prophet who performed symbolic, prophetic actions as well, like miraculous healings, cursing the fig tree, and cleaning out the temple to reveal the nature of his coming kingdom and the end of the old-world order.

Unwittingly, Jonah is acting out a prophecy, much like these other prophets did. Jonah in the sea and the fish is a sign of what is coming in Israel's future. It is an enacted prophecy of judgment upon Israel. Jonah's sin is Israel's sin; Jonah's plunge reveals Israel's inevitable judgment.

How do we know this is what is going on? To see this, we must make this connection between Jonah and his people more explicit. Jonah is a representative of Israel in this story. Jonah's role in the story reveals Israel's place at that time in history. Jonah is in sin and does not want to bear witness to the nations. He does not want to take the blessing promised to Abraham to the nations. Israel, as a whole, is in sin as well, and her sin is the same as Jonah's: the refusal to bear witness to the nations around her. She is hiding her lamp under a bushel and refusing to be the means through which God's light shines into the world.

Jonah is cast into the sea and Israel is going to be cast into the sea as well—the sea of exile. Throughout the Bible, the sea, as well as great sea monsters (like this great fish), serve as symbols of the Gentile nations, just as the land is symbolic of Israel.[2] Jonah is cast

---

2   On land/sea symbolism, see James B. Jordan, *Through New Eyes* (Nashville: Wogelmuth and Hyatt, 1985). The raging sea is a symbol of Gentile powers in numerous texts, including Isaiah 17:12 and 57:20. Sea monsters are symbols of Gentile rulers in several passages, including Psalm 74:12-17, Jeremiah 51:34, and Revelation 13:1-10. Israel is associated with the land for obvious reasons. The land of promise is her special home. Jonah is the only "sea story" in the Old Covenant prophets and, not surprisingly, it concerns ministry to Gentiles. Old Covenant prophets were typically involved in land-oriented vocations (e.g. Amos 1:1), but in the New Covenant, Jesus calls fishermen, engages in sea travel, eats fish, and so on. Paul also is a sea voyager. The change of venue points to a redemptive historical shift from a Jewish-focus to a world-focus. Of course, in Jesus, land and sea, or Jew and Gentile, are united (cf. Rev. 10:5-6).

into the sea and Israel is going to be cast into the sea as a pagan empire overtakes her, as she is driven away from her land into exile. But then God provides a great fish to keep Jonah safe. God preserves Jonah amid the sea and will do the same for Israel. The covenant nation will be kept intact, even through the exile. God will hold Israel together even in the belly of Assyria and Babylon.

Finally, Jonah is spat back out onto dry land and is restored to his prophetic calling (2:10). Again, this is just what will happen with Israel. The exile will come to an end, and there will be a new exodus and a restoration. Israel will return to her land. Jonah lives out the exile and return—or the death and resurrection—that the nation of Israel as a whole is going to undergo. This same point is made at the end of the story of Jonah, where God provides a plant to provide shade for Jonah to protect him from the blazing sun (4:6). In the same way, God will provide Assyria, a Gentile empire, to cover over Israel for a time.

Israel's Purpose in Redemptive History

To put all these puzzle pieces together, we must keep our eyes on the box top of the entire Old Testament narrative. We must seek to understand Jonah (the book and the man), considering God's design and Israel's purpose. Why did Israel exist? Why had God set them apart from all the other families and nations of the earth? We find the answer to this question in Genesis 12, where God initially chooses Abraham. God blessed Abraham to be a means of blessing to all the other families of the earth. And yet, again and again, Israel refused to shine the truth of God's glory and promises into the darkness of the nations of the world. All too often, she became just like those nations in her idolatry and unfaithfulness.

In a sense, we can think of Israel as God's mailman.³ What do mail carriers do? They deliver messages from a sender to their intended recipients. That is what Israel was supposed to do: deliver God's message to all the nations of the earth. But Israel acted like a mailman who pretends that all the mail in the bag is for him. Israel acts as though she has a monopoly on God's blessings. This is the great sin of Israel that leads to the exile, and it continues to be the great sin of Israel throughout her history, down into the first century, even into the days of Jesus and Paul—this insistence that the blessing is only for Jews. In the Book of Esther, the Jewish queen Esther conceals her identity instead of bearing witness to the pagan court. According to Paul's Letter to the Galatians, the Judaizers tell Gentile believers they can have Abraham's blessing, but only if they become Jewish first. In self-righteous pride, Israel arrogates herself to exclusive possession of divine truth and favor instead of seeing herself as a steward called to share these gifts with others.

In the Book of Jonah, Jonah eventually makes it to Nineveh, almost despite himself. When he gets there, he preaches and again, it seems to be a one-sentence message and a sentence of judgment no less! Jonah declares that in forty days, Nineveh will be overthrown (3:1-10). But how does Nineveh respond? Predictably, with repentance. Their reversal from idolatry to serving Yahweh matches the sailors' conversion back in chapter 1. The king of Nineveh affirms that perhaps God will show mercy on them instead of judgment if they repent. The king's hunch was right: God relents when he sees the change of heart in Nineveh. Of course, this also confirms Jonah's worst fears (4:2-3).

---

3   N.T. Wright notes that "election was never about Israel being called for its own sake, but always about God's call of Israel to be a light of the world... It is as though the postman were to imagine that all the letters in his bag were intended for him." N. T. Wright, *Bringing the Church to the World: Renewing the Church to Confront the Paganism Entrenched in Western Culture* (Minneapolis, MN: Bethany House Publishers, 1993), 39

All these things that Jonah had acted out come to pass. Within 50 years (likely within a generation of Jonah's death), the Assyrians came and conquered Israel, taking the covenant people away into exile (approximately 722 B.C.). Yet after some time, Israel returned from exile (approximately 536 B.C.).[4] Israel underwent the death of exile, but that death was followed by a resurrection. She returned from the sea of exile to her land.

Jonah is a sign to Israel—a sign of coming judgment that God was taking His word from the rebellious and hard-hearted nation of Israel and giving it to Gentiles who would receive it. Jonah's story of death and resurrection, exile and return, of being swallowed up by the fish and then being spit back out onto dry land reveals Israel's future. That would have been the immediate application of this book to its first audience. It is a book of warning and woe but also of future hope and victory.

JESUS AND JONAH

In Matthew 12, Jesus pushes us to an even deeper reading of the Jonah story. Jonah's story is Israel's story, but Israel's story, in turn, becomes Jesus' story. Jesus compares his own ministry to Jonah's and, by implication, his generation of Jews to Jonah's generation of Jews. He says the only sign he will give this generation is the sign of Jonah. So, we must ask: how are Jesus and Jonah and their respective ministries related?

---

4 For the sake of simplicity, I am using the standard, received (at least among conservative Bible-believers) chronology in William Hendriksen's *Survey of the Bible* (Grand Rapids, MI: Baker, 1995). See p. 233 on Jonah: "When Israel rejected Jehovah—as we learned from the prophecy of Amos—Jonah was commissioned to carry the word of God to Nineveh, the capital of that very nation which was even now expanding its boundaries until, after about half a century, it would destroy the kingdom of the ten tribes! The prophet, probably fearing that Jehovah would transfer his love from Israel to Assyria, disliked his commission and boarded a ship which sailed in the opposite direction from Nineveh."

Jesus draws one obvious parallel—Jonah's being cast into the belly of the fish and then being spit out on the third day foreshadows Jesus' being buried in the belly of the earth and on the third day coming forth in the resurrection. But there is also a difference. Jesus is not simply a recapitulation of Jonah; he is greater than Jonah. There is correspondence but also escalation. And when Jesus undergoes his death and resurrection, it is not for himself. It is not merely for his own sake, and it is certainly not for his own sin. Instead, it is on behalf of the covenant people. Jesus suffers exile, not because he is forsaking his calling the way Jonah did, but because he is fulfilling his calling.

The meaning and context of Jonah's three-day-and-three-night sequence undergo a transformation in Jesus. But the key is to see that the pattern is the same: what Jonah underwent as an unfaithful Israel, Jesus undergoes as a faithful Israel. Jesus, like Jonah, undergoes exile; like Jonah, he descends into Sheol, into the jaws of death, the place of the dead (Jonah 2:2; Acts 2:31). But on the third day, he experiences an exodus when he comes forth from the grave in new power and experiences a great deliverance. He returns to the land of the living, just as Jonah did. He is renewed and restored.

There is a further link to explore. There are only a few other places in Scripture where this third-day theme occurs. We could look at the binding of Isaac's story, which uses the third-day motif for the death and resurrection (figuratively speaking) of Isaac (Gen. 22; Heb. 11:19). We could look at the Joseph story later in Genesis (Gen. 40; 42:17-18); or the ceremonial system, as the third-day theme emerges from time to time connected with symbolic death and resurrection.

But perhaps the most significant third-day passage in the entire Old Testament scripture is found in a prophecy from a contemporary of Jonah, the prophet Hosea. When Hosea speaks of Israel's coming exile, he says this:

> "He has torn, but He will heal us; He has stricken, but He will bind us up. After two days, He will revive us; on the third day He will raise us up, that we may live in His sight" (6:1-2).

Introduction

For Hosea, the whole period of exile is symbolically a three-day period. Israel is in a pagan grave for three days but comes forth revived on the third day. Of course, the Old Covenant Israelites would not have missed this connection with Jonah and his experience.

In I Corinthians 15, Paul summarizes the Gospel this way: "Christ died for our sins according to the scriptures.... He rose again the third day, according to the scriptures." But what Scriptures does Paul have in mind? What Old Testament texts gave this prophetic blueprint that included a three-day death and resurrection? It is precisely in these prophecies of Israel undergoing the death of exile and then the resurrection of the new exodus—these passages we find in Hosea and Jonah. Paul projects the nation's destiny onto Jesus so that Jesus embodies Israel in Himself and fulfills Israel's purpose. In a much greater way than Jonah, he is Israel's representative. He gathers up Israel's story into himself and lives it out, bringing it to its God-ordained climax and conclusion.

All that went before Jesus was type and shadow; Jesus is the reality. All that went before him was merely the blueprint, but Jesus has erected the building itself. In Jesus, Israel has definitively undergone the curse the nation deserved. Jesus experienced the supreme curse of exile in his death on the cross—exiled from the community (Mt. 26:31,75), from the city (Heb. 13:12), even from God himself (Matt. 27:46). But then a new Israel comes out the other side of this death, through Jesus' resurrection, entering the life of the age to come and life of God's promised eschatological blessing. Jesus brings to realization and fulfillment all the promises and hopes that the prophets held out to Israel. His resurrection constitutes a new Israel—an Israel that includes Gentiles, the very people Jonah was so eager to exclude.

Jonah as History

The typology of the Jonah story offers remarkable insight into the hermeneutic of the text. Yet, scholars have attempted to remove the story itself from the pages of history. If modern scholarship can keep Jonah only as an ancient piece of writing, they do not have to deal with the moral implications of the book. However, there are significant reasons to read Jonah with the confidence of its veracity guiding the ethical implications and the hermeneutical significance of the book for the overarching flow of redemptive history. There are several reasons for believing that the things recorded in this book, including even the great fish that swallowed Jonah and spat him out on dry land, happened within the arena of history. How and why do we make this claim?

First, the story reads just like any other historical narrative in the Old Testament. It has the same patterns and features, the same basic form and style that other historical records of the Old Testament display. The book offers no indication that it is merely a parable or fictional allegory.

Second, Jesus himself cites the book as though it were historical. Jesus speaks in Matthew 12 of that generation of Ninevites who repented at the preaching of Jonah. They will rise up on judgment day to condemn that generation of Israelites. But they will only be raised up at the end of history if they lived within history. For Jesus, the whole story of Jonah was grounded in actual events. Jonah and the Ninevites are regarded as historical personages, just as Solomon and the Queen of Sheba. According to Jesus, Jonah was a real prophet who preached and the Ninevites were real people who repented. The whole story has historical meaning to it.

Third, if we are looking at a fabricated story, then there is a crucial ethical problem with this book, especially with the book's writer. We know that Jonah, the son of Amittai, was a real person.

Introduction

We know that he was a historical figure from II Kings 14, whose name appears in a clearly and indisputably historical work. If the book of Jonah is indeed a made-up story about the prophet of Jonah, then it is an evil book because it attributes all kinds of sin to a prophet of the Lord. In the book of Jonah, we see the prophet disobeying God, speaking disrespectfully to God, and becoming angry and impatient. If Jonah, the prophet of the Lord and the son of Amittai, did not do any of these things, then to make up a story that says that he did and put it in historical form is quite slanderous. By analogy, if the historical Jonah did not do these things attributed to him in the book of Jonah, then this story has no place in the canon of Scripture. It belongs in the garbage can with other slanderous writings.

Finally, we have the testimony of church history. From the church fathers, all the way through the medieval period and the Reformation, right up to the rise of modern rationalism, the Church is virtually unanimous in accepting the events of Jonah as hard-edged history. In fact, in many cases, the historicity of the book is tied to the gospels, since Jesus described himself as a greater Jonah and compared his three-day stay in the belly of the earth to Jonah's three-day stay in the belly of the great fish.

Augustine, the great early church theologian, once got a letter from a friend asking, "How can we expect pagans to believe this story of Jonah and the fish that swallows him and holds him for three days and then spits him back out on dry land and he lives through all this?" Augustine's friend was questioning the historicity of the book in the face of pagan challenges. Augustine wrote back and said this: "The answer to this is belief must be withheld from all divine miracles or there's no reason why this should not be believed. I find it very astonishing that you set down the incident about Jonah as incredible unless you think it's easier for a dead man to be raised from the tomb than for a living man to be preserved in the belly of a great beast."[5] For Augustine,

---

5 *From Nicene and Post-Nicene Fathers*, First Series, Vol. 1, trans. J.G. Cunningham; ed. Philip Schaff (Buffalo, New York: Christian Literature Publishing

if you deny Jonah, how can you affirm Jesus? If miracles can happen, then there is no good reason to doubt the historicity of the book. If miracles cannot happen, then, of course, the whole Gospel unravels. If God can rescue Jesus from the grave, then He can rescue Jonah from the fish.

Another great church father, Jerome, pointed out that this was not the greatest of biblical miracles. If you claim to believe the Bible, this is not the greatest miracle that Scripture calls on you to believe. You have got to believe that three young men were put in a fiery furnace and came out without even smelling like smoke. You have to believe in a floating axe head. You have to believe in dead people being raised up from the grave. So, if you are going to reject the story of Jonah, then you might as well get out your scissors because you have got a lot of other passages in Scripture to cut away as well.

Cyril of Jerusalem, yet another church father, spoke of Christ's resurrection and Jonah's fish this way: "If the former is credible, so is the latter. But if the latter is incredible, so is the former."[6] Jesus and Jonah go together. There is no consistent way to confirm the historicity of Jesus' resurrection, on which the whole faith hangs, and then turn around and deny the events in the book of Jonah.

We could survey other examples from church history, but this is sufficient to make the point. There are weighty and powerful reasons for taking Jonah to be a historical narrative. To not do so is to break with the catholic Christian tradition.

Co., 1887.)

6   *From Nicene and Post-Nicene Fathers*, Second Series, Vol. 7, trans. Edwin Hamilton Gifford; eds. Philip Schaff and Henry Wace (Buffalo, New York: Christian Literature Publishing Co., 1894.)

Introduction

Jonah as Prophecy

Jonah is history, and we must affirm that in the face of an unbelieving, secularized age. We must be willing to be fools for Christ. This text is not a fairy tale or legend. But we also need to go beyond the mere record of history. While Jonah is not less than historical, it certainly is more than barely historical. Jonah is a prophetic book. It is grouped with the other prophetic books in the canon of Scripture for a reason. This observation is crucial because there is only one sentence of explicit prophecy in this book, and that one sentence of prophecy does not even come true (3:4). Nonetheless, Jonah is a prophetic work, and we have already suggested previously how this is so. Jonah is a "sign" (Mt. 12:39). As we have seen, the sign of Jonah is complex, composed of a pattern of events that happen first in Jonah's own day in a proleptic fashion and then in Jesus' day in eschatological form.

The book is prophetic, first of Israel's exile into the belly of the Assyrian empire and then her return to the land of promise. Jonah's whole ordeal, being swallowed up by the fish and then being regurgitated back out onto dry land, is a picture of what is to come in Israel's history with the exile and the new exodus. But at a greater level, the whole story is prophetic of Jesus. This is why Jesus described himself as one greater than Jonah. The entire episode with the fish and the three-day and three-night stay in the Sheol of the fish's belly is prophetic, pointing ahead typologically to the death of Jesus. Like Jonah, Jesus will descend into the belly of the earth and rise again on the third day. The narrative is history, but it is also a symbolic prophecy of things to come. It is history telling us what happened in the past, but it is also a prophecy, revealing the future.

Jonah has something else in common with the other prophetic books. The prophets went around critiquing Israel's sin, and Jonah does this as well. The real thrust of the book is a prophetic critique of Israel's pride and Israeli nationalism. The Jews were the chosen people of God, but they were to remember that their election was not an end. Instead, their election was a means to an end. This was clear back in Genesis 12 when God first chose Abraham and said, "I will bless you and make you a blessing to the nations." But at this point in history, Jonah is a typical Israelite. He is a fit representative of the nation at this time in history. Jonah wants God to be a respecter of persons. He wants Israel's unique place in history to be permanent, not temporary.

As the story unfolds, we find Jonah entrenching himself as an unfaithful prophet because he idolizes his own nation. He repents temporarily in the belly of the fish and stays repentant long enough to deliver the message. But at the end of the book, he is right back where he started. He wanted to protect his nation at any cost, even if it meant forsaking his prophetic calling. If being a prophet meant going to Nineveh and extending God's grace to unclean Gentiles, Jonah would only go if dragged there against his will.

Jonah as Literature

The prophetic nature of Jonah's book is also a literary masterpiece. At times, the most concise works of the Bible carry the most significant literary import. This short book is structured in chiasms. Those chiasms aid us in our interpretation of the book. But rather than focus solely on the chiastic structures in the book of Jonah, it is fruitful to examine other literary features of the book. In particular, it is remarkable to consider the humor and irony that the writer invests in this small work. Some of it is comic irony, intended to make one laugh. Some of it is a tragic irony, designed to agitate the readers or perhaps even make them weep.

The story contains countless incongruities. Things are not the way they are supposed to be. There is so much irony in this book that the entire story can be read as a satire. The book holds up Jonah's sin (and in Jonah, Israel's sin) to be ridiculed and mocked. Jonah is made into a laughingstock in this book, and, of course, Jonah is to serve as a mirror in which Israel would see how ridiculous her own pride looked. Humor is one of the best ways to attack something. If we can make someone laugh at themselves, we have won the battle with them. When Jonah is read properly, it becomes a seriously funny book.

Most of the humor in the book is very ironic and, therefore, subtle. Consider that Jonah is told by the Lord to arise and go east to Nineveh. Instead, he arises, goes west to Joppa, and boards a ship going further west to Tarshish. He is told to go one way, but he goes in the exact opposite direction. Plus, God said to go up to Nineveh and yet again and again in the first chapter we are told that Jonah went down. He went down to Joppa, down into the ship, down into the fish, down into Sheol. He is continually moving in the opposite direction (west and down) of the way God commanded (up and east).

On the other hand, the Gentiles in the book do arise. They do what Jonah was supposed to do—they go up. While Jonah is going down, the captain of the ship arises and, in fact, calls on Jonah to arise as well. Just as the Lord calls on Jonah to arise and preach, so the captain calls on Jonah to arise and pray. Later on, the king of Nineveh will arise; he will come up from his throne in order to put on sackcloth and ashes in repentance. So while Jonah is going down, these Gentiles are going up. These directional markers have symbolic value, ironically reversing expectations.

There is another piece of irony in the book: Jonah does not want to convert Gentiles, so he flees. But on the ship he says one sentence to these Gentile sailors and by the end of the chapter, they have all repented. This is a sign of things to come for Jonah. In Nineveh, he says one sentence to the people, and it is not exactly a sentence calculated to inspire hope; yet again, the people repent. Throughout the book, we find a building contrast between God and his mercenary servant. God is slow to anger and full of compassion, while Jonah is quick to anger and full of hatred. The Gentiles are a much better reflection of God's own character than Jonah is. In fact, at the end of the book, we find that Jonah cares more about the death of a plant than he does for the death of 120,000 people in the city of Nineveh! But compare that to the sailors in the first chapter of the book. They were so concerned about the life of this one disobedient prophet that they risked their own lives trying to row back to shore instead of immediately throwing him overboard with the cargo.

Jonah celebrates God's mercy when it is given to him. He rejoices when God rescues him in the fish, and he is delighted by the plant that provides shade for him. But when that same mercy is extended to others, he becomes angry enough to die. Further, Jonah identifies his God to the sailors as the Maker and Lord of land and sea. But, then if Jonah's God made the sea, why is he fleeing from him by way of the sea? Jonah knows that there cannot be any escape from the Lord. He knows the Lord will hunt him down.

Perhaps the greatest ironies of all center on Jonah's preaching in Nineveh. We would expect a preacher to rejoice if his message were met with complete repentance from the top of society down to the bottom. Everybody in Nineveh, from the king down to the animals, repents. Many other prophets warned their hearers about coming judgment in vain. Many other prophets would have given anything to have success like Jonah experienced in Nineveh. Some have observed that Jonah is Israel's only successful prophet. But Jonah's response is antagonistic to God's purposes. Jonah's "success" makes him mad at God.

There are many other literary features in this book, but this sarcastic irony is at the heart of the book's message. Because Jonah represents Israel, the book is a parody of Israel in her sin. It is an ironic parody of Jonah's pride, and therefore, of Israel's pride, and it can be of our pride as well if we do not strive for humility.

Introduction

Dating and Context of Jonah

We learn from 2 Kings 14 that Jonah was from the region known as Gath Hepher. This was part of the territory that Joshua had originally assigned to the tribe of Zebulun. But Zebulun never drove out all the Gentile inhabitants, so this region in northern Israel was always mixed. It became known, in fact, as Galilee of the Gentiles, a largely Gentile region. Jonah was accustomed to living and ministering to Gentiles. An ancient Jewish tradition even tells us that Jonah had a Gentile mother. The Jewish rabbis believe that Jonah was the son of the Sidonian widow in 1 Kings 17, whom Elijah raised from the dead. Whether that is true or not, we can be sure that Jonah did not have some irrational fear of Gentiles. When he rejects the Lord's command to go to Assyria, it is certainly not because he wants to avoid all contact with non-Jews. That would not have been possible in the region of Gath Hepher anyway. Instead, it is because he does not want to play any part in extending God's mercy and strength to the nation that is most threatening to Israel at this time in history, to the empire of Assyria. Jonah knew the Torah, which taught that Israel had provoked the Lord to jealousy by going after other gods, and now the Lord would, in turn, provoke Israel to jealousy by taking his word and his presence to another people, to the Ninevites. The conversion of Assyria would be the beginning of the end for Israel, and Jonah knew it.

We also learn from 2 Kings 14 that Jonah ministered during the reign of Jeroboam II. This detail puts Jonah roughly in the mid-700s B.C. Now, Israel was wicked at this time, a reflection of their wicked king, Jeroboam. And yet we see that God was very merciful to Israel. God blessed them despite their sin, it seems, so that His goodness might lead them to repentance.

We often look at judgments from God as a way for how God will lead us to repentance. But Romans 2 tells us that God's goodness, good gifts, and blessings are intended to lead us to repentance as well. God gave unparalleled prosperity to the northern kingdom at this time in history. He rescued them from their oppressors not because they deserved it but so that they would turn to him and love him. Jonah prophesied that Jeroboam would restore the boundaries of Israel to what they had been during the glorious reigns of David and Solomon. Almost certainly, Jonah's prophecy inspired Jeroboam to seek to reclaim these lost regions. About a generation or so earlier, the Syrians had devastated Israel. Still, now Israel would regain her power if she drove out the Syrians and took back her lost territory.

Israel's reprieve in Jeroboam's day turned out to be very short-lived. Because Israel would not repent in times of blessing, God took the blessing away. He took his word and presence to another nation and sent Assyrians to conquer Israel within another generation. We must see that the goodness of God—every bit as much as the judgments of God—are intended to lead us to repentance.

The events recorded in the book of Jonah take place after the prophecy made in 2 Kings 14, probably even after Jeroboam has restored this lost territory to Israel. By the time the Lord sends Jonah to Nineveh, he is a veteran prophet, a seasoned prophet who has had prophecies come to pass. He is, indeed, a man of God.

1

Repentance unto Life

Jonah 1:1-16

¹ Now the word of the Lord came to Jonah the son of Amittai, saying, ² "Arise, go to Nineveh, that great city, and call out against it, for their evil has come up before me." ³ But Jonah rose to flee to Tarshish from the presence of the Lord. He went down to Joppa and found a ship going to Tarshish. So he paid the fare and went down into it, to go with them to Tarshish, away from the presence of the Lord.

Jonah as Dove

Who is Jonah? We find an initial indication in his very name. The name Jonah means *dove*. Throughout Scripture, we find doves associated with the Holy Spirit. In Genesis 1, the Holy Spirit flutters down above the watery earth. The word used for flutter or hover is a word used for birds flapping their wings to fly. In Genesis, it appears the Holy Spirit has proceeded out of heaven to earth and is now like a hovering bird over this watery mass that the Lord will go on to form and fill over the six days of creation. There are other references to doves in Scripture. After the flood, Noah sends out a dove. This time we find the dove hovering above the floodwaters, looking for the dry ground in the new creation.

Further, at the baptism of Jesus, we see the Holy Spirit descending out of heaven in the form of a dove to hover above the waters of the Jordan, finally landing upon Jesus, who is Himself the new creation incarnate.

Does Jonah's name mean he is a bearer of the dove-like Holy Spirit? Or should we take his name as ironic? Jonah is not very dove-like in this story. If anything, he is an anti-dove figure as he seeks to flee from the Lord's presence and reject his prophetic call. He does not hover above the waters; he is submerged in them. The irony continues with Jonah's family connection. Jonah is the son of Amittai. Amittai is Hebrew for the *truth*. Of course, the problem is that the only prophecy Jonah makes in the book is that Nineveh will be overthrown in forty days—and that does not come to pass! Again, his name has a touch of irony. Dove son of Truth is anything but dove-like and he does not seem to be very much of a true prophet either.

The calling of Jonah was precise: Arise and go to Nineveh. Nineveh was one of the great cities of the ancient world. The word *great* is one of the narrator's favorite adjectives in this story. The author uses the word repeatedly to describe the wind and the storm that God sends upon the sea and the fish that swallowed Jonah. The greatness of Nineveh refers not only to the magnitude of the city but also to the city's importance to God. God cares for this great city.

The book presents Jonah as a zealous nationalist caring only about Israel. Love for nation is a virtue, of course, but it is possible to turn one's nation into an idol. Given the way Jonah elevates loyalty to his own nation above obedience to God's missional purposes, it is safe to say he has crossed the line into an idolatrous form of nationalism. In contrast to Jonah, God in this book is presented as the great internationalist who has compassion on all peoples. Yes, He has chosen Israel and set Israel aside as His special priestly people, but that does not mean that God has no compassion for the other nations. And indeed, God wants Israel to share in that compassion toward the other peoples of the earth. God does not desire to obliterate national distinctions but ultimately to sanctify every nation. The only other city called great in the Bible is Jerusalem, the holy city itself (Rev. 21:10). God is showing the same concern for Nineveh that He shows for Jerusalem. Jonah knew that God sent him to Nineveh as an agent, not of wrath, but of grace. Jonah was to bring Nineveh into God's blessings.

Jonah's Failed Rationale

Verse 2 informs the reader of the wickedness of the city. The wicked aroma of the city ascends before the Lord as though the city is offering a foul-smelling sacrifice. In the Bible, when nations present hideous and foul offerings, God intervenes with judgment. Nineveh is introduced as a place ripe for destruction. Nineveh is the capital of the emerging world superpower of the day, Assyria. And like so many other cities, it was a city full of wickedness and depravity on every street corner. How wicked was Nineveh? Sometimes we forget how brutal, raw, and evil unbridled paganism is. In our culture, we have not experienced true paganism; the Gospel's impact on culture over the last two thousand years has tamed and domesticated paganism in all kinds of ways. The influences of God's grace that have been operative in our culture for so long have had salutary effects, even on non-Christians. What theologians call "common grace" is just the spillover of special (or saving) grace. It is the residual influence of special grace in a culture. Non-Christians in our culture may reject the Bible and the Gospel, but they cannot escape the Bible's influence and the Gospel in our culture. Our cultural heritage in the West includes the Gospel, and it has kept our culture from societal death for some time. Whether this remains for much longer is an open question.

It was not this way in ancient Assyria. Ancient Assyria had never been the recipient of the saving grace of God. It was probably a wicked city from the very beginning. Truly pagan cultures are unspeakably horrific, and Assyria was no different.

After a military victory, the ancient Assyrian emperor would put giant fish hooks in the mouths of the vanquished and march them down Main Street in a victory parade. He would then impale them, lifting their skin off, and after skinning them alive, he would cut off their limbs and throw them to the wild animals to be devoured. That is what paganism looks like when it has not been mitigated in any way by the grace of God.

When the word comes to Jonah, the reader expects the usual biblical pattern for prophets, but Jonah has his own itinerary. As a prophet, Jonah is to be a council member, called to announce the divine council's message to the people. But Jonah fails to fulfill his prophetic duty as a participant of God's divine council. He decides to forsake his calling; instead of traveling by land to Nineveh, he will travel by sea in the opposite direction. Thus, the prophet proceeds to go down to the port city of Joppa to get on board a ship. God told him to go up, northeast to Nineveh, but instead, he went down, southwest to Joppa. He pays the ship's fare and gets on board a ship headed to Tarshish, located way out at the end of the Mediterranean Sea.

Jonah is not avoiding the mission to Nineveh because he thinks it is a lost cause, but because he knows it is a cause that will bear fruit. He knows the power of the Gospel, and consequently, he knows what might happen to Israel should God transform Nineveh. Jonah was called to cry against Nineveh, but in doing so, his warning implicitly offers the Gospel of peace to the city.

In fleeing, Jonah foolishly thought he could evade God's reach. But he should have remembered the words of the psalmist: "Where can I flee from your presence? If I am in Sheol, you are there!" (Ps. 139:8) God would not let Jonah run away from him and his calling to Nineveh, no matter how far he went.

> [4] But the Lord hurled a great wind upon the sea, and there was a mighty tempest on the sea, so that the ship threatened to break up. [5] Then the mariners were afraid, and each cried

out to his God. And they hurled the cargo that was in the ship into the sea to lighten it for them. But Jonah had gone down into the inner part of the ship and had lain down and was fast asleep. ⁶ So the captain came and said to him, "What do you mean, you sleeper? Arise, call out to your God! Perhaps the God will give a thought to us, that we may not perish." ⁷ And they said to one another, "Come, let us cast lots, that we may know on whose account this evil has come upon us." So they cast lots, and the lot fell on Jonah. ⁸ Then they said to him, "Tell us on whose account this evil has come upon us. What is your occupation? And where do you come from? What is your country? And of what people are you?"

⁹ And he said to them, "I am a Hebrew, and I fear the Lord, the God of heaven, who made the sea and the dry land." ¹⁰ Then the men were exceedingly afraid and said to him, "What is this that you have done!" For the men knew that he was fleeing from the presence of the Lord, because he had told them.

Jonah's Manipulation

In verse 4, God hurls a storm down on the sea and the sailors become filled with fear. In verse 5, each man begins crying out to his own god for rescue. These men belonged to a polytheistic culture. In many ways, twenty-first century American culture has become polytheistic as well, and we see the same kind of response whenever our culture faces a crisis: everyone cries out to his own God. Any culture that rejects the worship of the true God will end up polytheistic. Men will worship idols, and because no one of these idols is absolute, there must be several gods. There must be different gods for different geographic regions or gods of different activities. The god of this or that is the religion of humanity in Adam. Fallen man, as Calvin says, has an idol factory in his heart. Man is not so much *homo sapiens*, thinking man; ultimately, he is at his root *homo adorans*, worshipping man. As humans, we have this basic impulse to worship, to look for something transcendent. Man instinctively knows that since he is made in God's image, he ought to thank and glorify his true Creator and Sustainer. But because of sin, he twists and suppresses this natural knowledge of the true God and instead worships a god of his own devising (Rom. 1:18-32). We see this idolatrous impulse play out in Jonah 1, but with a surprising twist.

The stormy sea for the pagans is like a dragon-figure that swallows them whole. So, they are saying: "Please quiet this dragon! Make the sea stop roaring!" The pagans knew that Jonah was the reason for such maritime anger. The pagans possessed enough common grace to grasp the consequences of Jonah's disobedience to Yahweh. But Jonah is playing a manipulation game. He thinks that perhaps if God sees that he is not interested in the job, God will change his mind about the mission. The captain, however, sees through Jonah's rationale. The captain refers to Jonah as a sleeper. This description indicates that Jonah is not interested in helping others amid a dangerous situation, as the sea grows more and more tempestuous (1:11). Manipulation will not work with God. Sleeping, no matter how deep, will not change the plans of God. Jonah should have reasoned with God as Abraham did in Genesis 18 since interceding on behalf of the nations was part of Israel's mission.

[11] Then they said to him, "What shall we do to you, that the sea may quiet down for us?" For the sea grew more and more tempestuous. [12] He said to them, "Pick me up and hurl me into the sea; then the sea will quiet down for you, for I know it is because of me that this great tempest has come upon you." [13] Nevertheless, the men rowed hard to get back to dry land, but they could not, for the sea grew more and more tempestuous against them. [14] Therefore they called out to the Lord, "O Lord, let us not perish for

this man's life, and lay not on us innocent blood, for you, O Lord, have done as it pleased you." **15** So they picked up Jonah and hurled him into the sea, and the sea ceased from its raging. **16** Then the men feared the Lord exceedingly, and they offered a sacrifice to the Lord and made vows.

The Sailors' Response

When the sailors hear Jonah's confession in verse 9, they respond by becoming even more afraid. Jonah announces that he is a prophet of the one true Creator God. Suddenly, the sailors find something more terrifying than the storm. In verse 4, it says they were afraid of the storm, but in verse 10, after hearing of Jonah's God, they became "exceedingly, greatly" afraid. They are now face-to-face with the Lord. They have now heard about God with a capital "G," and they now know that their idols are nothing.

The text indicates that these sailors repented of their idolatry by offering sacrifice to the Lord. These sailors were willing to turn from their idols to the living God, and in this way, they are more exemplary for us than the prophet Jonah. The Christian life is continually turning from idols to offer sacrifices of service and praise to the living God.

There is a specific application of this principle in the Epistle of 1 John. The Apostle addresses a believing community, giving them assurance that God loves them and that they are in true fellowship with him. And yet this 105-verse letter ends with this warning, seemingly dropped into the letter out of nowhere: "Beloved, keep yourselves from idols" (I John 5:21). The letter's emphasis is living in vital fellowship with Jesus Christ, and yet it concludes with this reminder to avoid idolatry. John was well aware that believers can turn from Jesus Christ to other gods, even if it is ever so temporary. Every time a Christian sins, he is serving another god. The Christian's call is to constantly fight against idolatry. This endeavor is not a one-time thing, as though a person can repent from idolatry and be done with it forever. Instead, the saint must continually fight against idolatry. Our hearts are prone to wander, and so we must fight to remain true to the true God, without compromise. We must pull the plug on the idol factory in our hearts and not let it get cranked back up again.

In verse 6, the captain approaches Jonah, awakens him, and calls on him to pray. The captain is still thinking like a polytheist at this point. He wants Jonah to pray, so they will have all their bases covered. But the sailors soon find out by casting lots that Jonah is the root of the problem; his disobedience is the cause of the storm. Jonah suggests that if they want to stop the storm, they should throw him overboard if they want to appease the Creator God.

The first response of the pagan mariners is to fight Jonah's advice to throw him to certain death in a watery grave. They do not want to be guilty of innocent blood, so they endeavor to row back to shore. But it is all to no avail. The storm is simply too strong for them. At this point, we must interject something vital to our overall understanding of the story. We must see how highly ironic this is. These pagan sailors have just heard about the God of the Hebrews, the God of Israel, and yet they show more compassion toward Jonah than Jonah, the Israelite, shows toward them. Jonah closes his heart toward them, even though the Old Testament law, again and again, commands the Israelites to show compassion toward foreigners and to be a light to the nations. He refuses to even pray for them, refusing to play Israel's role as a nation of priestly intercessors. Jonah does not pray until he ends up in the belly of the fish. We have already noted Jonah's hard-heartedness toward the Ninevites. At this stage, these pagan sailors show more concern for one disobedient prophet who has put their lives at risk than Jonah shows for a city of 120,000 who do not know their right hand from their left. He would rather die than preach to the Ninevites and play some part in their salvation. He will sacrifice himself to his idol.

Moreover, his action of fleeing from the Lord's presence renders his confession hollow. If he fears God, why is he running from him rather than obeying? If he knows that God made the land and the sea, why is he trying to escape by way of the sea?

There is a vast discrepancy between his creed and his actions. His flight betrays his words and his words mock his flight. He is, in short, a hypocrite. And yet the sailors do their utmost to try to save him.

Finally, in verse 14 they cry out—but this time, they cry out not each to his own god, but to Jonah's God. Ironically, they are now on the path to repentance, even though Jonah remains unrepentant. They acknowledge that while Jonah may be a hypocrite, his God is the true God, and in sending the storm, he was only doing what pleased him. They acknowledged his sovereignty over the creation and his justice in sending the storm to track down his runaway prophet. Finally, after saying, "Lord do not hold us accountable for the death of an innocent man," they throw Jonah overboard. They hurl him into the sea, just as they had previously hurled the cargo of the ship overboard, just as previously the Lord had hurled down the storm upon the sea. And verse 15 tells us that as soon as they did so, the sea ceased from raging. It is as though as soon as Jonah touches the water, instantly the storm stops and the dragon ceases to roar.

THE FRUIT OF REPENTANCE

Repentance plays an essential role in the theology of Jonah. At times, we see the normal expectations shattered since instead of Jonah repenting, the Gentiles become exemplars of repentance. Jonah's story offers a rich understanding of repentance, summarized with at least three observations.

First of all, the storm alone did not make them repent. The sailors needed Jonah's confession of the truth. And even though Jonah himself was not living up to the truth that he spoke at that stage, the Lord made his word effectual. Suffering all by itself is never enough to turn a person to the Lord. The individual must hear the word of truth. Jonah's confession enabled the sailors to connect the dots to see the real reason for their suffering. In *The Problem of Pain*, C.S. Lewis says God whispers to us in our pleasures, speaks to us in our conscience, but shouts to us in our pain.[7] Lewis says that suffering is God's megaphone, his wake-up call to rouse us. That is true enough. But we need to be careful to realize that suffering all by itself cannot change a sinner's heart. It may only make him more bitter. When God shouts to us in our pain, it must join with the shout of the Gospel through preaching (Is. 52:7) to lead the sinner to repentance. Only the Lord's sovereignty can make sense of our suffering. God may use the blows of his providence, but only his word can truly transform and rebuild us.

But there is a second aspect to notice about their repentance as well. We have already analyzed the anatomy of idolatry, but we need to examine the anatomy of repentance as well. If idolatry is creating a God-substitute, repentance is substituting God for the idols. Repentance restores god to His rightful place in our lives. Repentance means acknowledging that this God is the Lord over all the lesser gods we previously served. Repentance means changing our allegiance, abandoning loyalty to false gods and our affection for them, and directing all our worship to the true God. Hence, everything else in life falls into place under his Lordship. We must never think of repentance apart from faith. Repentance is just the back side—or perhaps the front side—of faith. Repentance is turning from idolatry; faith is turning to the living God.

The Westminster Shorter Catechism (Q87) teaches that repentance demands grief and hatred of sin but also an "apprehension of the mercy of God in Christ." No one repents without first believing that God is merciful. No one repents without first coming to love God more than they love their sin. No one repents without finding God and His promises more attractive than the lies of idols. The Bible and the Westminster Standards are not being legalistic when they teach that repentance is necessary to receive the forgiveness of sins. The demand to repent is not legalistic; it is gracious through and through.

---

7   C.S. Lewis, *The Problem of Pain* (1940; repr., San Francisco: HarperSanFrancisco, 2001), 91.

Repentance is "unto life," as Westminster puts it; it is a saving grace. Repentance means we must face our idolatry, forsake the false gods and fight them. And because our old idols never leave us alone, we must never stop repenting. Martin Luther, a major figure in the sixteenth-century Reformation, is probably best known for his teaching that justification is by faith alone, the truth that spearheaded the Protestant Reformation. But the first of his "95 Theses" characterized the entire life of believers as one of repentance. Luther understood the whole Christian life was to be permeated with repentance as a continual turning away from sin to embrace the Lord's mercy.

But the most crucial aspect of repentance is that it gives rise to worship. The return to worship is the third and final feature of the story of Jonah's interaction with Gentile sailors. Verse 16 says, "Then the men feared the Lord exceedingly, and they offered a sacrifice to the Lord and made vows." Note the progression. In verse 5, they became afraid because of the storm. Now the storm has gone away—yet they have an even greater fear. They fear the Lord more than they fear the storm. They fear more after the storm is over than they did at the height of its raging. Fear in the Bible is often synonymous with reverence; when fear is directed toward the Lord, it is even synonymous with worship. John Calvin, the sixteenth-century French Reformer in Geneva, says as much when he writes, "the fear of the Lord means a sincere desire to worship God."[8] In biblical language, faith is a part of *fear*. To fear God means seeing Him and embracing Him as a sovereign father. The Christian needs a God who is sovereign and powerful enough to help His people, yet one who also is a faithful and loving father, determined to do good to His people. The fear of the Lord recognizes both of these truths. This is why a true fear of God drives believers to worship God instead of driving us away from him. When we think of something that we fear, we

---

8   John Calvin, *Commentary on the Prophet Isaiah* (Grand Rapids, MI: Baker Book House, 1998 reprint), 375.

think of something to flee from. But here it is just the opposite: we are drawn to him if we fear him. That is why it is so ridiculously foolish for Jonah to stand up and say, "I fear God," when he is trying to run away from God's presence instead of running into God's presence.

At the end of chapter 1, the sailors come to fear the Lord, and as a result, they offer sacrifice and make vows. Perhaps they offered sacrifice right on board the ship, or maybe they went to the temple in Jerusalem later (cf. Numbers 15, which makes provision for Gentiles offering sacrifice at the tabernacle). We do not know the details since verse 16 ends the role of the sailors in the story. The focus in verse 17 shifts back to Jonah and stays with him for the balance of the book. But, again, note how ironic the whole story has already become: Jonah did not want to be a missionary to the Gentile city of Nineveh, and so he fled, but he inadvertently ends up converting these Gentile sailors who no doubt will become missionaries in their own way as they sail all over the world telling people about the Lord God of Israel, who rescued them from the storm.

It is only fitting that this story of the sailors that began with idolatry should end with worship. True worship is the ultimate antidote to idolatry and the primary purpose of our creation as image-bearers. Idolatry enslaves and dehumanizes us, but true worship frees us and re-humanizes us. The worship of the Lord is the most human thing we can do.

2

The Psalm of Jonah: Salvation Is of the Lord

Jonah 1:17-2:10

Jonah must have known his Bible very well because his prayer in chapter 2 is a patchwork of pieces from upwards of 20 different Psalms. It is a lovely mosaic drawn from fragments taken out of the Psalter. The song is a veritable echo chamber of other biblical prayers and hymns. Jonah has pulled together various lines and phrases from the Psalter and recombined them into a new Psalm appropriate to his new situation.

Each one of these Psalm-pieces in Jonah 2 has a string attached. We could follow that string back to its original context and deeply enrich our understanding of Jonah 2. For example, several phrases in Jonah 2 allude back to Psalm 18. If we looked at the traces of Psalm 18 that Jonah grafted into his prayer, we could come to a deeper understanding of Jonah's intentions as he enters into conversation with the psalmist David. By listening for the resonances and echoes of other Scriptures, we could unlock doors to Jonah's prayer that otherwise remain closed to us. This kind of intertextual exegesis is simply using Scripture to interpret Scripture in a rigorous way.[9] As necessary as this exegetical task

---

[9] For an excellent example see, Richard B. Hays, *Echoes of Scripture in the Epistles of Paul* (New Haven: Yale University Press, 1989).

is, we will not undertake that project. Instead, we will consider the overall form and structure of the Psalm and then look at its theology and application.

Praying in Bible-speak

¹:¹⁷ And the Lord appointed a great fish to swallow up Jonah. And Jonah was in the belly of the fish three days and three nights.

²:¹ Then Jonah prayed to the Lord his God from the belly of the fish, ² saying,

"I called out to the Lord, out of my distress,
    and he answered me;
out of the belly of Sheol I cried,
    and you heard my voice.
³ For you cast me into the deep,
    into the heart of the seas,
    and the flood surrounded me;
all your waves and your billows
    passed over me.
⁴ Then I said, 'I am driven away
    from your sight;
yet I shall again look
    upon your holy temple.'
⁵ The waters closed in over me to take my life;
    the deep surrounded me;
weeds were wrapped about my head
    ⁶ at the roots of the mountains.
I went down to the land
    whose bars closed upon me forever;

The Psalm of Jonah: Salvation Is of the Lord

> yet you brought up my life from the pit,
>> O Lord my God.
> ⁷ When my life was fainting away,
>> I remembered the Lord,
> and my prayer came to you,
>> into your holy temple.
> ⁸ Those who pay regard to vain idols
>> forsake their hope of steadfast love.
> ⁹ But I with the voice of thanksgiving
>> will sacrifice to you;
> what I have vowed I will pay.
>> Salvation belongs to the Lord!"
>
> ¹⁰ And the Lord spoke to the fish, and it vomited Jonah out upon the dry land.

As just noted, virtually every word of Jonah's psalm comes from the Psalter itself. And yet, this is not just a copy of any particular Psalm. Instead, when Jonah talked to God on his own, the language of his heart flowed out in the language of the Psalter. Someone said of John Bunyan that the Bible was in his blood so that when you pricked him, he bled Bibline. He could not speak without quoting the Bible. Similarly, Jonah could not pray without relying on the Bible's language. If you pricked him, he bled Psalter.

How was Jonah able to pray in the language of the Psalter? How did he get these biblical prayers into his spiritual bloodstream? Certainly, Jonah had an advantage over others in ancient Israel in that he was a prophet. He was literate and probably had easier access to the Scriptures. In our day, all Christians are prophets in the sense that the Holy Spirit teaches us as we spend time studying and meditating on the Scriptures so we can speak biblical truth into our world.

But there is something else that stands behind Jonah's biblical fluency. From his youth, Jonah would have participated in liturgical services at the temple and in the local synagogue (Lev.

23:3). In these services, the Scriptures were central to corporate worship. The Scriptures would have been read in large portions and the Psalms would have been sung extensively. Bits and pieces of the Scriptures would have been used in corporate declarations and responses (e.g., the Shema of Deuteronomy 6). Through this liturgical and disciplined form of worship, Jonah (and other Israelites) would have imbibed the Scriptures deeply.

This is the genius behind liturgical worship (when carried out well). It creates a corporately memorized tradition. Liturgical, ritualized worship makes the Scriptures a part of the worshipper, pressing the word of God down into the very fabric of his being. Once shaped by the liturgy, even spontaneous prayers end up sounding a lot like the psalmist or the Book of Common Prayer. Perhaps we may know people who are so steeped in the language and forms of the psalms that their prayers were almost indistinguishable from the biblical psalter.

The overflow of Jonah's heart expresses itself in the words of Israel's liturgy. Jonah opens his mouth and God's own words come out. But they are now his words because he has soaked himself in the Scriptures for so long. Likewise, our prayers should come to effortlessly mimic the psalter's beauty, depth, richness, and vitality. Through participation in liturgical worship forms, constant reading and meditation on the Scriptures, and sustained practice in communal and solitary prayer, we can develop prayer habits that enable us to pray the way Jonah prays in this chapter.

The Psalm of Jonah: Salvation Is of the Lord

Structure and Flow

This psalm is a literary and theological masterpiece. This entire episode of Jonah is a very carefully crafted piece of literature. This passage that runs from 1:17 through 2:10 is structured chiastically:

    A. The fish swallows Jonah (1:17)
        B. Jonah petitions God for salvation (2:1-2)
            C. Jonah descends to the abyss, yet looks to the Temple (2:3-4)
                D. Jonah's "death and resurrection" (2:5-6)
            C.' Jonah ascends from the abyss, knowing his prayer went up to the Temple (2:7)
        B.' Jonah praises God for salvation (2:8-9)
    A.' The fish spits Jonah out (2:10)

A chiastic literary structure has matching sections, beginning with the outermost pieces, usually called the brackets, that envelope the passage. Then, as we move inward, there are matching sections that interpret one another, until we finally reach the center of the structure, which is the most critical part of the passage. The center of the chiasm gives the theme of the chiastic block.

In 1:17, the fish swallows Jonah; at the end of the passage in 2:10, the fish vomits Jonah out onto dry land. Moving inward, in 2:1-2, Jonah calls on God to save him; in 2:8-9, he praises God for the salvation he has received. These sections match, giving us Jonah's prayer and the answer to his prayer. In 2:3-4, we find him descending into the abyss, yet he is looking up to God's temple. In verse 7, he is ascending from the abyss, and he says that his prayer rose to the Lord in His temple. Finally, right in the middle, in verses 5 and 6, we find the death and resurrection of Jonah. This section is truly the center of this entire narrative: Jonah's descent into death and his resurrection and deliverance. The prayer points to the Lord's salvation as He rescues Jonah from Sheol. Jonah goes down into death, and he comes up into new life.

The Location of the Prayer

Before we dig into this psalm, there is a problem with this passage that we need to consider, namely, its timing. When did Jonah offer up this prayer? Of course, we might be tempted to say he offered up this prayer when it was too late. And that, indeed, would be true. We know that Jonah should have been praying to the Lord long before this. Perhaps you have heard the old joke: A crisis hits a church so one Christian says to another, "I guess we ought to pray." And the other Christian says, "Has it come to that?" All too often, we make prayer our last resort, just as Jonah does here. We need to be dropping to our knees to pray as our first response to a crisis, not our last response.

The question concerns the timing and location of Jonah's prayer. When does Jonah pray this prayer in verses 2-10? If we look at this prayer carefully, we will find more thanksgiving than petition. Much of the language that Jonah uses makes it sound as though he has already been delivered. Considering this fact, some commentators (including John Calvin) have suggested that the prayer offered in the fish's belly in verse 1 is a different prayer than the one recorded in verses 2-9. In verse 1, he prayed from the fish's belly and then after he was rescued, he prayed the prayer of thanksgiving recorded in verses 2-9. Perhaps this explains the past tense and the thanksgiving within the prayer.

However, the most natural reading of the text indicates just one prayer. The sequence is quite clear: In verse 1, Jonah prayed in the belly of the fish, and then we are given the content of that prayer in verses 2-9. In verse 10, the fish spits him back out onto dry land. Jonah must have composed this prayer of thanksgiving even while he was still in the fish's belly. Jonah must have figured out what the Lord was up to in preparing and providing the fish. Jonah discovered that the Lord did not complete His work in him and that he would receive a second chance to fulfill his mission.

Jonah realizes even from the depths of the great fish's belly that God will give him a clean start and a new opportunity to obey. By faith, the prophet speaks of his deliverance and even gives thanks while still in the belly of the fish. This point will turn out to be quite crucial in the passage.

Swallowed Up Into Sheol

There are two ways we need to approach this passage. First, we want to do a low-altitude fly-by overview, stopping just long enough to pick up on some key details. Then, we will pull back to look at the "big picture" in terms of the psalm's major theological themes. We will see the central theme of God's sovereignty in Jonah's death and resurrection and several sub-themes that cluster around that main theme.

Consider first the details as we work through the text verse-by-verse. In 1:17, the Lord appointed a "great" fish to swallow this runaway prophet. Later, we will find the same word being used as God appoints a plant, a worm, and a hot wind from the east. The same term is used to describe God's control of his creation in each one of these cases. God is the omnipotent Lord over the works of His hands. But we need to be careful how we understand God's sovereignty. God's sovereignty is not a matter of raw power. Instead, He is the servant-king of creation. Everything in the creation is at His disposal, of course, since He is the creation's comprehensive master. But at the same time, He is the absolute servant of creation, continually working on creation's behalf to sustain it and energize it. Thus, He not only appoints the fish, but He also prepares it. Biblically, we should say God is creation's absolute Lord and Ruler because He is creation's Servant and Sustainer. Biblically, power and service are not opposites but coordinates. Creation can only do God's bidding as God enables it to do so.

The word used for *swallow* in 1:17 shows up in several other places in Scripture. For example, it appears when the earth swallows up the wicked family of Korah (Num. 16). It shows up again in Exodus 7 when Aaron's snake swallows up those of the Egyptian magicians. In context, the term carries the connotation of suddenness, even of judgment. To be swallowed up would not seem to be a very good thing. And indeed, at first, Jonah sees the fish as an affliction. In verse 2, he cries out to the Lord during his distress because of this great disaster. As Jonah moves through his prayer, however, he comes to see the fish as a blessing disguised as a catastrophe. He discovers God has appointed the fish as a means of salvation.

The fact that Jonah prays indicates he is finally responding to the chastening of the Lord. Things cannot get any worse for Jonah, but he finally pulls out of his despair and turns to the Lord in expectant faith. However, this does not mitigate the trauma of the experience. He says his cry came out of the belly of Sheol (2:2). It seems the fish becomes a kind of watery tomb for Jonah. He experiences a form of death in the fish.

Sheol, of course, is the underworld, the realm of the dead. It is where all the deceased went, both righteous and unrighteous, in the old creation before Jesus opened up heaven to the saints. When Jesus ascended into heaven, He became the first man to fully enter into God's sanctuary-throne room (Rev. 4-5). Now, heaven is open to all those who have trusted in God's mercy for salvation. Indeed, we enter heaven in some mystical way even before death in prayer and worship (Heb. 4:16; 10:19ff). Heaven is also the abode of the righteous dead as they await the bodily resurrection and the new earth. After Jesus entered heaven, He transferred the old covenant saints to heaven with him (Ps. 16:10; Eph. 4:7-10; Heb. 11:40; Rev. 1:18; 6:10; 15:1-8). Now, He also takes us there when we die (2 Cor. 5:1-8; Phil. 1:21).

Sheol is never depicted as a desirable place in the Old Testament, even though it is seen as the place where everyone goes when they die. Jews rightfully saw Sheol as a terrible place. Death was a dreaded enemy because it removed one from the land of the living, out of your family and community, the places where God's blessings could be found. In the Greek worldview, of course, Sheol—or Hades, as they called it—was a person's final destination at death. For the Greeks, this was the soul's "hope"—to shed the prison-house of the body and live forever as a disembodied soul. There was no hope of a resurrection. There was no hope of "life after life after death," as N.T. Wright has put it.[10] There was no hope for a renewed physical creation.

The Jewish hope is very different—very earthy, very bodily. This is why a descent into Sheol was so unwelcomed by Jonah. Death and disembodiment were enemies because they took a person out of God's good creation. The ultimate Jewish hope— and of course, it is the Christian hope as well—was not losing the body in death, but getting the body back in the resurrection and being restored to one's place on the (renewed) earth (I Cor. 15:53).

So, when Jonah speaks of going down into Sheol, we should understand this as a very unpleasant experience. This is Jonah's worst nightmare. We do not know if Jonah literally died in the fish (it is certainly possible given other persons who undergo a death and resurrection in Scripture) or if he is just speaking metaphorically. Whatever the case, it is clear that the fish becomes a grave for the prophet.[11]

But if the belly of the fish is death for Jonah, then coming forth from the fish will be a resurrection. His expulsion from the fish is his return to the land of the living. He goes to Sheol and back in the narrative—or to hell and back, we might say. Jonah goes

---

10   N.T. Wright, *Surprised By Hope: Rethinking Heaven, the Resurrection, and the Mission of the Church* (New York: HarperCollins Publishers, 2008), 151.

11   There is a possibility that Jesus' audience in Matthew 12:40 would understand the *ketos* as a sea serpent. This interpretation would open up new realms of interpretive possibilities, since serpents function as death-representatives, especially in the garden narrative of Genesis. Thus, Jonah is swallowed up by death itself.

down into Sheol, but the gates of hell did not prevail against him for long. The Lord burst those gates open, and Jonah returned from the land of no return.

Jonah acknowledges in verse 3 that it was not ultimately the sailors who cast him into the sea. Rather, the Lord himself has done this. Jonah knows that God works through creaturely agencies, like the storm, the sailors, and the fish. He recognizes that his fate is not in the hands of some pagan sea god, nor is he left to the blind forces of nature. In his psalm, he acknowledges that the Lord God of Israel purposed his predicament.

Jonah says the flood waters of the storm and the sea surround him. The flood language recalls the great deluge in Genesis 6-9. It is as though he has been kicked off Noah's ark and the waves of judgment are crashing upon him. It is as though he is left to drown in the fury of God's wrath. The language and the imagery echo the flood narrative, making Jonah into an anti-Noah. Jonah is not on the ark; he has been cast out and left to drown.

The Resurrection of Jonah

In verse 4, we start to see a change of heart in Jonah, and therefore a change in his situation. He has been steadily descending, moving farther and farther away from the Lord's heavenly presence. Chapter 2 fills out a theme that began in chapter 1 where he goes down to Joppa, down into the ship, down into the lowest parts of the ship, down into the sea, down into the fish's belly, down into Sheol or the underworld, even down to the roots of the mountains. That is about as low as you can go! Since special, revelatory events happen on mountains (e.g., Mount Moriah, Mount Sinai, Mount Zion), to be taken down to the roots of the mountains is to get as far from the place of blessing as possible.

But now, he looks up to the Lord's Temple. The Lord has cast him out of His sight, but now Jonah begins looking to the Lord's heavenly dwelling place. He is at the roots of the mountains, but he looks to the mountain of the Lord. When he begins to sense that the Lord has lost sight of him, he begins to look to the Lord. And from the lowest place in the earth, his prayer begins to rise to the Lord in heaven.

Interestingly, Jonah mentions the temple. Does Jonah have in mind the temple in Jerusalem or the Lord's heavenly temple? Biblically, the one is a shadow of the other. The temple in Jerusalem is not only the location where God dwells among his people; it also is "heaven on earth," the place where heaven and earth come together. Jonah looks to the temple because he knows whence his help comes (cf. Ps. 121:1). The temple calls to mind God's mercy because it is the place of confession, sacrifice, and cleansing. It is the place where God's mercy is made available in the means of grace and where the people go to meet with God, renew covenant with him, see, hear, and feel his forgiveness.

For Jonah, looking to the temple is a sign of repentance. Earlier, he fled from the Lord's presence, seeking to escape his prophetic calling, but now his heart turns back to that place where the Lord is most especially present. He wants to be back in the Lord's presence in the temple. In short, we can say that Jonah prays to the temple because Jonah repents of his sin.

As Jonah looks to the Lord, the Lord stretches out His arm from the temple to deliver him. Verses 5-6 include details indicating the interpretive category through which Jonah understands this deliverance. Jonah says that weeds (or reeds) are wrapped around his head. We have already seen an allusion to the flood story in verse 3; now, we see an allusion to the exodus narrative.

The word for *weeds* (or it may translate as "seaweed") is very unusual. It is the Hebrew word that occurs in the name of the Red Sea, which is literally rendered as the Sea of Reeds. Thus, the allusion indicates that the shape Jonah's salvation takes is a new exodus. Just as the Israelites crossed through the Sea of Reeds and came out on the dry ground, Jonah will come through the reeds that have wrapped themselves around his head and return to dry land (2:10). Just when it looks like Jonah is going to be another Egypt drowning in the Sea of Reeds, he comes forth as a new Israel, emerging from the sea reeds to dry ground. He escapes the reeds of the sea, just as Israel escaped the Sea of Reeds. To be even more specific, we can say Jonah became a new Moses in the belly of the fish. This same word is also used in Exodus 2 when baby Moses is hidden in the reeds. Moses and Jonah are both submerged in reeds when they are drawn forth from the water.

In verse 7, Jonah acknowledges that his prayer has made it to the Lord's presence in the temple. This second mention of the temple fulfills his desire expressed in verse 4. Again, note that the temple is where God sits enthroned above the cherubim on the ark of the covenant. It is something of a cosmic control center. God directs the universe from His temple, which is why prayer is directed to the temple—the temple is the place at which believers can lay hold of God's power. Several biblical passages identify the temple as a place from which God's redeeming power comes forth. We see this, for example, in the book of Revelation, where blessings and judgments repeatedly come forth from God's sanctuary. The prayers of the saints rise up before God in His sanctuary; God reaches out to deliver the saints from His sanctuary. Just as earthly kings make declarations and issue decrees from their throne rooms, so does the King of kings. This is what gives Jonah's prayer its power and efficacy. Prayer offered through faith reaches up to the Lord's throne room in the heavenly temple.

Verse 8 shows us what happens to those who continue to cling to their worthless idols (or it could also be translated "empty faiths" or "false religions" or "foolish vanities"): they forfeit the grace that could have been theirs. Jonah says idolatry is utter foolishness. It is possible that Jonah is referring to the pagan sailors who called out to their own gods amid the storm. But it seems more likely that he has his own false faith in view. As he was fleeing from the Lord's presence, he was committing a form of idolatry. He was recreating God in his own Jewish, nationalistic image. He was clinging to a false religion. Jonah repents of that, and in doing so, he claims the mercy God offers him.

In verse 9, Jonah announces the follow-through of his repentance. Having forsaken his idolatry, he will sacrifice thank offerings to the Lord and he will keep his vows. This is Jonah's way of acknowledging the ultimate truth that salvation is of the Lord. Indeed, this is the great climax to his prayer: an acknowledgment that salvation is the Lord's doing.

Salvation is the root word from which we get the name Joshua. It is also the word from which we get the name Jesus. It means "deliverance," but also "victory" or "triumph." Jonah's psalm, which begins with despair, distress, and desperation, ends on a note of victory and triumph. The Lord answers his prayer, so Jonah's psalm ends with this ringing declaration that salvation and triumph come from the Lord.

Finally, this section closes out in verse 10. The Lord commands the fish and it vomits Jonah out onto the dry land. The fish, unlike Jonah, obeys the first time he receives a command from God. Jonah's resurrection and salvation are now complete. A new Jonah emerges from Sheol. He now knows from experience what serving the God of land and sea is all about. He knows God now as the God of death and resurrection, as the God of exile and exodus, and as the God of judgment and salvation. Jonah has been rescued and now he will be re-commissioned. He will be restored to his calling as a prophet.

When we ask what this psalm is about, a clear answer emerges. The psalm is about the death and resurrection of Jonah showing forth that salvation is of the Lord. That is the center of the chiastic literary structure. But what does it mean for us? How can we make Jonah's psalm our own? We can draw five theological applications from this text.

Five Lessons from Jonah's Psalm

First, the Lord is sovereign in salvation. This lesson can never be overemphasized because even if our heads know it, our hearts can all too easily forget it. We are fallen sinners with no claim to

God's mercy. He is free to save who He wills and damn who He wills. God could have let Jonah drown in the sea or perish in the belly of the fish, and He would not be one whit less righteous or less gracious. God is God. He is the Potter and we are the clay—and none can say to Him, "Why have you made me thus?" God declares, "I will have mercy on whom I will have mercy, and I will harden whom I will harden" (Rom. 9:15, 20). He is sovereign in election, in choosing whom He will save; He is sovereign in accomplishing our forgiveness through the death of Jesus Christ on the cross; He is sovereign in reorienting our hearts, sending His Spirit to grant us faith and repentance and ensuring that we persevere in faith to the end. Every last bit of our salvation is His doing. There is no single link in the chain of salvation that we make with our own autonomous free will. It is all His work from beginning to end, from everlasting to everlasting. We can add nothing to God's work of salvation, any more than Jonah could do something to contribute to his salvation. Jonah was utterly helpless in the sea and in the fish, and we are utterly helpless in our bondage to sin. We are radically dependent upon the mercy of the Lord for salvation. Like Jonah, we must look to the Lord God alone for salvation. Salvation comes through the death and resurrection of the Greater Jonah, and in no other way. It is all His doing which we simply receive. We do not contribute to our rescue in any way.

But the second point we see—and this is not a contradiction of what has just been said—is that the Lord's salvation is conditional. If we are going to participate in this great, divine work of salvation, we must comply with certain conditions. There are certain things we must do. *Conditions* is not a bad word, neither are the words *obligation, duty, responsibility,* or *obedience.* Now, to be sure, we can only fulfill the conditions by grace, but we still must fulfill them. No one can do them for us. God works them in you, but He does not do them for us. We must act and repent turning from worthless idols and endeavoring to worship the Lord. We must turn from sin and endeavor to walk in new obedience by believing in God's promises and forsaking false gods. These are the conditions of the covenant.

God acts in His sovereignty to save Jonah, but He also only saves Jonah as the wayward prophet repents and re-enters the way of life. In this prayer, we find Jonah repenting and trusting the Lord's power to save. The whole story turns when Jonah begins to cry out to the Lord and ask for rescue and salvation. If Jonah did not pray this way, he would have perished in the sea (or, in the belly of the fish). Only when Jonah turns to the Lord and cries out in humility does the Lord stretch forth His mighty arm to bring about the great deliverance. Jonah meets the conditions of the covenant: faith, repentance, and prayer. We must distinguish between trying to earn something and the effort arising from a heart that loves and trusts God.

We discover what happens to those who reject the conditions of salvation in verse 9. Those who continue clinging to their idols, rather than repenting and trusting the Lord alone, forfeit the mercy that could be theirs. Mercy is truly offered to them. God offers salvation to all in the Gospel, but if we refuse to receive it with a repentant faith and insist on having it on our own terms, we will not receive it at all. Again, understand this carefully: To speak of conditions for salvation (or conditions of the covenant) is not legalistic. It does not throw the burden of salvation back on the believer's shoulders, as though, in the end, it all comes down to that person. Conditions do not suck the grace out of the Gospel, as though they implied a believer must save themselves in the end. That is not the case in Jonah's situation! To reiterate, we can only fulfill these conditions as God's grace enables. We work out what God works in us (Phil. 2:12-13).

The conditions point us to the way of life and salvation. That is to say, God's free salvation comes to us as we walk in this path of faith and repentance. And what is faith? It is simply acknowledging our utter dependence upon the Lord for salvation.

It is trusting in Him to work it out for us and in us. Repentance means turning from sin to trust in Him and to walk in the way of obedience.

We must understand that the commands of God and the covenant conditions are good news. When God told Noah to build an ark, He was issuing a command. But that command was designed to show Noah the way of life. God did not tell Noah to earn his own salvation. But if Noah did not build the ark, he would not have been saved when the flood came. By believing and obeying, Noah met the covenant conditions and was saved in the ark. All of God's commands—the command to worship Him alone, the command to honor father and mother, the command to avoid lust, the command to not steal or to not covet, and so on—are simply commands to build an ark. This is the way of life and the path toward salvation.

Third, because God is a Father to those He saves, He chastens us. He is the hound of heaven, relentlessly and lovingly pursuing His wayward child. The Lord tracks Jonah down, first with the storm, then with the fish. He will not let one of His children get away without a fight. He keeps striving with us and working with us to bring us to repentance. And when He catches us, He chastens us to train us in holiness so we will stay closer to the path of righteousness in the future.

Biblically, all of the suffering we go through as children of God is to chasten us. In this way, it serves our good and conforms us to the image of Christ. All the pain that God brings into our lives amounts to the Lord's loving discipline. Sometimes we must go through quite a bit of suffering to learn our lessons. Parents know this, which is why they may use the rod and repeatedly rebuke to correct a child. Just when it seems like he is never going to learn, he does! Because we love our children, we are relentless with them. We continue to pursue them with discipline and refuse to hand them over to their sin. And this is just what the Lord does with us.

Verses 3-5 show us the intensity of the Lord's discipline. Jonah has seaweed wrapped around his head and the water is surrounding him. The waves are washing over him as he sinks down. This is a picture of a drowning man. It is not a pretty picture, but it is a picture of a man under the Lord's discipline. To raise a child, sometimes a parent must make a child feel like they are trying to kill him. And sometimes, as the Lord raises us up in the way we should go, it feels as though He is trying to kill us. But the pain is all part of His larger loving purpose.

To receive the Lord's discipline in the right way, we must follow Jonah's example and respond to it in faith and repentance. We must understand that the point of His discipline is not just to make us take our lumps, nor is it to make our lives miserable. Instead, it all has this one supreme purpose: to make us like Jesus Christ, who learned obedience from suffering. The point is not that God wants to beat us up; the point is that God wants to make us holy. And so, we must pay attention to what He is doing in our lives and learn from it.

Jonah learns this lesson, and he repents. After he makes it back to dry land, he fulfills the original mission by going to Nineveh and preaching to them, and they repent. But by chapter 4, the Jewish prophet is right back where he started. He has slid back right into the same sin. And the Lord is going to have to discipline him again, this time using a scorching heat and a strong wind to correct Jonah. But it is the same thing; the Lord keeps working with Jonah, just as He keeps working with us.

Cotton Mather, the great Puritan, put it well. In describing the necessity of parental discipline he said, "Better whipped than damned." In other words, it is better to be shaped by the rod than go to hell. This is the teaching of Proverbs: "You shall beat him with a rod, and deliver his soul from hell" (23:14). God handles His children as the model Father. When it feels like God is beating the hell out of us, well, He is! Or, to be more precise, God is beating the hellishness out of us. Just as He beat the Sheol out of Jonah, so He beats the hellishness out of us. But of course, He does this so we will not suffer in hell for all eternity. We are given a taste of hell in this life, so we will not taste it in full in the afterlife. The Lord's painful discipline bears the sweet fruit of repentance.

Mather's point that we are "better whipped than damned" is fully biblical. Those are our only choices: the Father's whip or the fury of hellfire. If we grasp this by faith, this warning gives us an encouraging way of grappling with life's pains and mysteries. Just as we discipline our children in love, so does our heavenly Father. Hebrews 12 says that this discipline is a mark of our sonship. It may be painful for a while, but it serves a good purpose in our lives.

The discipline of the Lord is proof that we belong to His family and are under His care. So, the disciplining hand of the Lord in our lives is a good thing. It is not meant to dishearten us; it is meant to transform us. And we need to receive the blows that the Lord inflicts upon us in this light. We need to see this as the loving hand of God upon us. The afflictions and trials that He brings into our lives are intended to cause us to cry out to the Lord in repentance. Jonah was disciplined and he repented. The Lord is disciplining us, and we must repent as well.

Fourth, we see that this salvation comes through means. God does not just zap individuals with a lightning bolt of salvation from out of the blue. Rather, God works through means. God's salvation comes to us through His ordained means within the covenant community. In verses 4 and 7, Jonah looks to the Lord's temple, and that is when salvation comes to him. The temple is the place where God dwelt, but of course, that was not all. The temple was also the place where the word of God was found and where the Ten Commandments were housed in the Ark of the Covenant. It is the place where sacramental, sacrificial meals were celebrated. It is the place where the covenant people gathered for worship to receive God's gifts and offer Him gifts in return. It is the place where the people met for covenant renewal.

Suppose we were to ask, "Where is the Lord's temple today? Where are these functions performed for us? Where can we go to find a word of forgiveness and the special 'temple presence' of the

Lord? Where can we go to share a meal with God and His people?" For us, of course, all these things are found in the church, which is the new and true temple of God (cf. Eph. 2:11ff; 1 Pet. 2:4ff). In the new covenant, if we desire to renew the covenant with the Lord, we do not make a journey to Jerusalem. We do not look to an earthly temple. Instead, we come to church to gather for Lord's Day worship. The Church is where God is present to meet with us and bless us. It is also the place of salvation and victory when we remember the Lord as our prayers are offered up and answered.

American Christians have tended to pry the church—the temple of God—from the salvation of God. Many have driven a wedge between these two, as though salvation is over here and the church is over there. For example, some may say the church is a friendly help to aid us along the way in our personal spiritual journey, but it is by no means essential. We are so individualistic and afraid of anything that smacks of what we might think of as a dead formalism in worship that we dislike authority structures. We tend to think that if we were really holy we can do without all of these external crutches. Looking to the church/temple, as Jonah did, is either something relegated to the old covenant era or is treated as a retreat back to Romanism. We think that the new covenant brought in a spiritual relationship with God, a spiritual form of religion that is all inward, individualistic, and private. Because of all these things, we come to disdain the church.

But this simply is not true. This argument does not hold up when we look at it in light of Scripture. The church is not an oxygen tank or pacemaker that weak Christians need, but strong Christians can do without in their lives. As John Calvin said, "You never outgrow your need for mother church."[12] We need to understand, as the church fathers and Reformers did, that ordinarily, there is no life or salvation outside of the church (Westminster Confession of Faith 25.2). Just as there was no life or

---

12 John Calvin, *Institutes of the Christian Religion*, Book Fourth. "Of the Holy Catholic Church," trans. Henry Beveridge (Grand Rapids, Michigan: WM. B. Eerdmans Publishing Company, 1989), 2279ff.

salvation to be found outside of Noah's ark, so there is no salvation or life to be found outside of the church. Just as for Jonah, there was no other place to look for help other than the temple of God, so if we want to find God's blessing, we must gather with His people and partake of the means of grace in faith. We too must look to the Lord in His temple, which is His church, seeking Him where He has promised to be found.

The church is the place where God is at work restoring creation and community. In the church, God turns idolaters to true worshippers. The church is where we begin to practice life as God intended us to live. The Spirit does not bypass the church or the means of word and sacrament in working his salvation. If He did so, salvation would have to take us out of the world and out of history. It would be a gnostic escape hatch. It would be a way out rather than a way of transformation. But that is not the picture that we get in Jonah or the rest of Scripture. For Jonah, salvation means restoration to the land and covenant community. God saves us, not by taking us out of the world or out of the family or out of the workplace; He saves us amid these relationships and structures and institutions and even begins to heal us and transform us by His grace. Yes, salvation means a break with the world—in the sense of the world's fallenness. Sometimes that will mean loss of job or family. But ultimately, God's plan is to restore created structures, not eradicate them.

But, again, how does this salvation come to us? It comes to us through the church, through the means of grace that God has ordained. And that is, indeed, why we gather each Lord's Day to receive the Lord's salvation anew. Word and sacrament are the power of God unto salvation for all who believe, the effectual means of salvation. Jonah looked for his salvation to come through the temple, and we must do the same.

Finally, these means of grace have a single end: sacrificial worship. In verse 9, Jonah says to the Lord, "But I with the voice of thanksgiving will sacrifice to you; what I have vowed I will pay. Salvation belongs to the Lord!" The end goal of all this is that Jonah would worship the Lord once again. God has saved, pursued, disciplined and rescued Jonah—all to this end, that Jonah might worship. This is God's chief end in saving us: to seek worshippers. God gives us deliverance and we give God the glory.

Of course, chapter 1 also ended with worship, so there is a parallel. The same language is used in 1:16 and 2:9. Chapter 2 tells us much the same story as chapter 1, but with a different people group. In chapter 1, Gentile sailors turn to the Lord; in chapter 2, a Jewish prophet is brought to worship. All of this is a typological foreshadowing of the new covenant when Jew and Gentile will worship the Lord together.

The truths taught in this chapter will be picked up by Paul and developed in Romans 3:21ff. Both the sailors and Jonah have fallen short of the glory of God, and both the sailors and Jonah can only be restored to that glory by faith in the mercy of God through Jesus Christ. There is no difference between the sailors and Jonah when it comes to sin and salvation. Both have fallen in Adam and worshipped idols. Both receive salvation in the same way through the same means in Jesus Christ. God is not only the God of Jonah; He is also the God of the sailors.

The parallels between Jonah 1 and Jonah 2 are too obvious to ignore. The sailors call to the Lord in their distress and Jonah does as well. The Lord heard the sailors' prayer and answered, just as He does for Jonah. The sailors acknowledge that the storm came from the Lord, just as Jonah recognizes that his predicament comes from the hand of the Lord. It was the Lord's storm in chapter 1; Jonah says it is the Lord's water and waves surrounding him in chapter 2. The sailors repent; Jonah repents. The sailors' story ends with worship, specifically with sacrifices and vows; this episode ends with a promise to offer sacrifice and pay vows as well. In both stories, redemption accomplished by the Lord creates an obligation to worship.

The application is clear: The Lord has rescued us through the sacrifice of Christ, and so we, in turn, are to honor Him with sacrificial worship. The Lord took us out of Adam and put us in Christ. The Lord has granted us faith and repentance and drawn us away from worthless idols to worship Him and caused us to seek Him in His temple. He has given us access to His heavenly sanctuary.

Everything in our lives serves the purpose of transforming us into true worshipers. God did not save Jonah so he could be a missionary. Everything is subordinate to worship, including missions. We evangelize only because the Father is seeking worshipers from every nation. Worship trumps missions. Worship trumps everything. Everything God does for us and in us is to make us into a worshiping community.

3

Nineveh Overturned: The Salvation of the City

―――― ～≈•≈～ ――――

Jonah 3

Jonah 3 is, at the same time, the easiest and the most challenging chapter in this book. Jonah goes to Nineveh and preaches a one-sentence sermon. The Ninevites repent, and in response, God does not follow through on His threat to destroy the city. Nineveh is spared by God's mercy, teaching us that the only way to avoid destruction and find salvation is by turning to the Lord in faith and repentance. It is a simple message.

Yet this chapter presents us with some incredibly complex theological questions to solve. Right from the start, the narrative shows us how complex God's providence is. First, God says He is going to destroy the city of Nineveh by turning the city into another Sodom and Gomorrah because of its great wickedness. But the Ninevites change their course of action, so God changes His course of action and relents from destroying Nineveh. How do we relate this act of relenting to the eternal decree? What does it mean for God to change His mind—and is that even possible? How can this story compare with other texts that teach God is not a man that He should repent or change His mind (I Sam. 15:29)? Didn't God change His mind about Nineveh? This chapter raises some perplexing questions.

Nineveh was the greatest city of the ancient world, the great political and economic superpower. No one would have been able to overtake the city of Nineveh at that time, and yet, God sends in an army of one man and sacks the greatest city in the history of the world up to that time! It is certainly a surprising event. It is also startling that this great revival involves one very reluctant, begrudging Jewish prophet and a horrifically wicked pagan city. But, again, this is not exactly what we would have expected. Why would God go to such great lengths to spare this one renegade prophet Jonah to save this multitude of undeserving Gentile sinners? Why Jonah? Why Nineveh? Why not, say, Isaiah and Jerusalem? Again, the story is simple but also full of surprises.

An additional problem raised in this chapter concerns the status of the Ninevites as Gentiles. If Israel is the chosen nation, why is God sending a missionary prophet to the Assyrians? Why do we see God sending a Jewish missionary to a Gentile nation in the Old Covenant? Could Gentiles experience precisely the same salvation that the Jews did in the Old Covenant order? Would the Ninevites have to be circumcised and participate in temple worship to experience that salvation? Again, more questions to consider.

Jonah 3

> [1] Then the word of the Lord came to Jonah the second time, saying, [2]"Arise, go to Nineveh, that great city, and call out against it the message that I tell you." [3] So Jonah arose and went to Nineveh, according to the word of the Lord. Now Nineveh was an exceedingly great city, three days' journey in breadth.

This chapter begins similarly to the beginning of the book. Once again, the word of the Lord comes to Jonah, telling him to go to Nineveh and preach. The words in the opening verses of chapter 3 are almost identical to the book's opening lines as a whole. But there is one noteworthy difference: in chapter 3, the text says that the word of the Lord came to Jonah a second time. That may not seem like a big change, but we have a picture of divine grace in those two words. God is the God of clean slates and new beginnings. God has mercifully acted to restore Jonah to the office of prophet. The story is getting back on track, thanks to God's grace. The story has taken a brief detour down to Joppa, down into the belly of the fish, and down to the bottom of the ocean. But now, God meets Jonah where he is, not where he should have been.

In 3:3, Jonah arose and went, according to the word of the Lord. He finally undertakes his prophetic task in the great city of Nineveh (cf. 1:2). The city's greatness is emphasized twice, in 3:1 and 3:3. In other words, this is an exceedingly great city. This "greatness" can refer to the size of the city or perhaps to the reputation or the military power of the city. But when we consider the way this language is used elsewhere in Scripture, we come to a slightly different conclusion. Greatness most likely refers to the city's significance but not in terms of political, economic, or militaristic might; instead, the term most likely refers to the city's place in the plans of God. The city was great in God's eyes because God was planning to use Nineveh for His own purposes. In a sense, Nineveh becomes God's chosen city. Earlier in Scripture, Gibeon is called a great city (Josh. 10:2). But most often, Jerusalem is the great city (e.g., Jer. 22:8; Rev. 11:8, 14:8, etc.). In some form or fashion, Nineveh becomes a new Jerusalem in the mind of God.

A Biblical Theology of the City

The whole flow of the story of redemption in the Bible is a movement from the garden to the city. The move from Genesis to Revelation is a move from Eden to the New Jerusalem. While city imagery in the Bible refers primarily to the church (which is the City of God and the New Jerusalem), it also has a secondary reference to our earthly cities. The church herself is to be the model city. Earthly cities are to be copies of the heavenly city that God is forming by the blood of His Son and the work of His Spirit. Thus, the church becomes a blueprint for other forms of community.

Cities at their best are, in fact, faint representations of the church. Cities at their best are places where the marginalized, the poor, the needy, and minorities can find shelter, work, and help. They are places of great cultural development and maturation. They are places where music, art, sports, cultural centers, trade, technology, and craftsmanship are all developing. Cities allow the blending of cultures and ideas like nowhere else. Cities become bodies in which all the parts work together to form a multi-functional whole.

Throughout history, the church has worked wonderfully to transform city life. Paul's early missionary efforts used cities strategically to spread the Gospel, as Acts shows. First, he would preach in the city of a region. Then, he would consider that region evangelized because he knew that if he captured the city for Christ, it would eventually trickle out to the rest of the surrounding regions. His letters address city churches in the major urban centers of the Greco-Roman world.

We can learn much from the early church in this respect. Paul concentrated his missionary efforts in cities because he knew that if the Gospel transformed the city's culture, the outer-lying regions would also be transformed. Thus, Paul addressed his epistles to city churches, as did Jesus in Revelation 2-3. While cities at their best are glorious, we are usually familiar with cities at their worst. Because cities have been deserted mainly by evangelical and Reformed churches, we typically encounter cities that fall far short of the Biblical blueprint. They are places of poverty, crime, oppression, corruption, pride, and violence. They are centers of idolatry where men gather, not to worship the true God, but to worship the idols of money, pleasure, and power.

Some of our own cities have become synonymous with rebellious lifestyles—think of San Francisco, Las Vegas, or New Orleans. Several cities in Scripture became symbolic of different forms of evil as well. The first city was built by Cain right after he killed his brother. That city was built on the sacrifice of Abel's blood. Fratricide became the foundation of Cain's city. Later in history, fratricide would become the foundation of Rome, as one brother killed another and erected the city on his brother's sacrifice. The city of Babel came to represent man in his defiance of God. The city/temple complex of Babel was constructed so that man could storm heaven and shake his fist in God's face. Similarly, Nineveh was an ancient city known for its wickedness, especially for its shocking violence and brutality. Nineveh became synonymous with evil and oppression in its day.

This story teaches two things concerning the city. First, this story shows us that however corrupt and wicked our urban communities may be, and however Nineveh-like they become, we should never give up hope in the mercy of God to change them. If God can make a city like Nineveh repent, surely He can make our city repent as well. Second, as bad as most of America's urban culture has become, we dare not write it off or give up on it.

These conclusions do not necessarily mean we all need to live in cities, but it does mean that God's people need to always have a heart for the cities since cities will always be strategic to spreading the Gospel and the transformation of culture. Cities reveal more about what a culture is like and where it is headed than anything else. The significant culture shapers are almost always found in cities. In a sense, if we want to know where American culture as a whole is going, all we have to do is look at our major cities. If we are going to disciple our culture, there is no better place to start than planting churches in urban areas.

The second point concerns the true hope of the city. What Nineveh needed (and what all cities need most) was not better school systems, better urban planning, better sanitation systems, better roads, or a Super Wal-Mart. All those things may have their place, but what this story teaches us more than anything else is that the only hope of the city is the mercy of God. Likewise, the only hope of transforming the culture of the city is the Gospel. Only the grace and mercy of God can beautify the city's life. City dwellers (and country-dwellers, too, of course) need to hear the

Gospel. Our hope for the city must be based on God's grace, not in politics, education, social services, or anything else, for only the grace of God can transform our cities and culture.

Nineveh's Problem and God's Solution

⁴ Jonah began to go into the city, going a day's journey.
And he called out, "Yet forty days, and Nineveh shall
be overthrown!" ⁵And the people of Nineveh believed
God. They called for a fast and put on sackcloth,
from the greatest of them to the least of them.

⁶ The word reached the king of Nineveh, and he
arose from his throne, removed his robe, covered
himself with sackcloth, and sat in ashes.

Nineveh was a great city in God's sight. Moreover, Nineveh was in great need of God's mercy. What does God do about Nineveh's plight? In verse 4, we find that Jonah begins to walk and preach his way through the city. He announces that in forty days Nineveh shall be overthrown. In verse 5, the people of the city respond with immediate repentance. Jonah had to be coaxed into obedience. Israel had been confronted with one prophet after another pleading with the people to repent though still they refused. However, the Ninevites get only one prophet (and not even a particularly obedient prophet, at that) and one sentence of prophecy (compared to books of prophecy for the Jews), and yet they repent immediately. The result is an instantaneous and dramatic change of heart.

As already noted, in verse 3, we are given some sense of the size of the city. It would have taken three days to make one's way through the city. Verse 4 states that Jonah began his preaching tour through the city, presumably taking three days. But immediately, the story cuts to the Ninevites' response in the next verse. It is as though the Ninevites repent before Jonah even finishes with his preaching itinerary; before the preacher can even finish his sermon, the people are rushing out to put it into practice.

The Ninevites did not hesitate when they heard the threat of divine judgment from this Jewish prophet. They did not sit around and critique the sermon; they did not just sit around and wonder what it might really mean for them. They took immediate action.

We might think that this response would be every preacher's dream. Surely any preacher would be thrilled if his preaching got this response! Yes, that is usually true for preachers—every preacher, that is, except for Jonah. We might think that a sinner saved by grace (like Jonah back in chapter 2) would rejoice to see other sinners saved by that same grace. But as we have already seen, this is precisely Jonah's existential struggle. Jonah resents having to share covenant privileges and blessings with outsiders and enemies. When he sees Nineveh, he sees a city full of enemies to be damned instead of sinners to be saved. When he sees the Ninevites start to repent, his worst fears come to pass. He has had a hunch as to why God sent him to Nineveh in the first place, and he rebelled against his mission because he wanted no part in saving and strengthening a rival nation. He is thinking exclusively in terms of his own nation and his people, rather than in terms of the kingdom of God, which is always bigger than our families or our nation. Jonah wanted a parochial God, not a God whose redemptive purposes are global. This is Jonah's attitude in this chapter, and it is still with him in chapter 4. It is a mockery of the God that Jonah professes to serve who is, as Paul says in Romans 3, not a God of the Jews only but a God of the Gentiles as well. Jonah wants to bottle God's grace up and confine its benefits for his own people.

When Jonah says in verse 4 that Nineveh is going to be "overthrown," or "turned upside down," he is using the same word used three times back in Genesis 19 to describe the judgment that God brought against Sodom and Gomorrah. The words of Genesis 19:21, 25, and 29 inform us that God overthrew

Sodom and Gomorrah. At this stage, God threatens Nineveh. The Assyrian capital is going to be turned into a pile of smoking rubble just as Sodom and Gomorrah were—at least Jonah hopes so. But the word itself can go both ways. It is not necessarily a negative word. For Nineveh to be turned upside down (right side up?) could mean a change for the better. If Nineveh was already upside down, overturning Nineveh would be a good thing. The Hebrew term is used this way in Esther 9:22, among other places. In Esther 9, the mourning of the Jews is "overturned" by God's grace; their grief is turned upside down into rejoicing when God grants them victory over their enemies. Thus, for Nineveh to be overthrown sounds ominous. But there is a subtle trace of hope in the declaration, thanks to the word's ambiguity. It sounds like judgment, but it could, perhaps, mean reformation.[13]

Jonah says that Nineveh's destruction will occur in forty days. Just as Jonah got a second chance, so Nineveh is going to get forty days. This sounds like a prophecy of sure doom, but the time block also means that there is time for God to reconsider. Nineveh might be on death row, but she has had a stay of execution. So why bother to wait unless God is open to rethinking His judgment?

The number forty in Scripture (in particular, *forty days*) is a symbolic period of time in Scripture. It is usually associated with a time of testing, judgment, or transition. For example, Israel wandered in the wilderness for forty years, transitioning from slavery to freedom. Of course, it was also a time of God testing

---

13 This further develops the contrast between what happens with the Ninevites and Israel. Jeremiah used the same language, saying that Israel would be overthrown. What response did he get to his preaching? The Jews did not exactly repent! Instead, they arrested Jeremiah and threw him into prison (see Jeremiah 26). Clearly the Ninevites are putting the Jews to shame. The Ninevites, by their response to this threat of judgment, are showing themselves to be true Jews, while the true Jews themselves are showing themselves to be false Jews because they refuse to repent when confronted with this same message. Jonah, thus, becomes a story of reversals. This whole story seems to have things backwards. It is as though everybody's identity has been switched around. Of course, this kind of gospel topsy-turvy becomes even more explicit in the NT.

His people (e.g. Exod. 17). Moses was up on the mountain for forty days at Sinai. It also was a test for the people, as they were forced to come to grips with Moses' extended absence. The spies were sent into the land for forty days to scope out Canaan doing reconnaissance work and gathering intelligence. It was a forty-day period of testing to see whether or not they would claim the land by faith or shrink back in unbelief.[14] The number *forty* in this story is not accidental, though it may be hard to pin down its symbolic significance. Perhaps it indicates that God's threat of coming judgment is a test to see how Nineveh will respond to the word of God. Will they ignore the warning or will they repent?

Verse 5 gives us a description of Nineveh's repentance. They responded by fasting and dressing in sackcloth. These are signs of mourning and contrition. The text says that this was a universal response on their part. From the greatest to the least, everyone had been sinning, so now everyone, from the greatest to the least, joins in this corporate act of repentance.

In verse 6, the king finally gets word of Jonah's preaching. The king, to his eternal credit, immediately joins his people in their acts of repentance. He gets up from his throne, acknowledging a new King, the God of Israel. He trades in his royal robes for sackcloth and ashes. To remove his robe is to remove his glory. He dethrones himself to sit in ashes as a sign of his death to his old ways. These responses signify great humility and indeed reveal a more godly response than many of Israel's kings.

Then, the king issues a decree. He gathers with his nobles and together they issue an official edict. This proclamation makes their spontaneous response of repentance the official political response of the city to Jonah's declaration. In effect, this pronouncement makes Nineveh a theocracy as the city is brought under the rule of the God of Israel.

---

14 There are other examples: Elijah's journey to Horeb took forty days, mimicking Israel's wilderness period; Goliath taunted the Israelites for forty days, challenging them to put someone forward as as warrior; and Jesus was tested in the wilderness for forty days, doing battle with Satan.

The Politics of Repentance

The king's response offers a symbiotic relationship between repentance and politics. As already noted, politics is never going to be the answer to our problems. It is often the cause of our problems. But at the same time, we need to acknowledge that civil government is ordained by God and political rulers can be forces for good (even if only minimally so). Rulers can help bring about cultural transformation and renewal if—and this is a big *if*—they are willing to genuinely and publicly repent, allowing God's word (as opposed to the word of man or the word of some vague, undefined, unoffensive god) shape their public policies and decision making. The Ninevite king sought the common good of his city and his empire by decreeing repentance. In our society, politicians would never talk about repentance because repentance is considered a private matter. For many people, repentance is a sectarian, rather than public, concern. Instead, our politicians will speak about fuzzy, generic virtues that everybody can agree upon (precisely because they are undefined). But in Jonah, we have a case of a bona fide biblical theocracy, as the king calls on the people to do something particular and biblical: he orders them to repent from their sin and serve the Jewish God.

Romans 13 says that civil rulers are God's deacons (or servants), and this king fulfills that vocation. He recognizes that he is the servant of a higher king, and he puts all his power, authority, and influence over his people at God's disposal. There is probably not enough in this text to develop a whole theology of politics or an entire philosophy of church/state relations, but we can use this material to make a start. As Americans, we focus a lot of attention on grassroots politics and reformation from the bottom up. That is all good and true. But in the Bible and throughout history, we also see reformation coming from the top down. Rulers cannot force true religion on their subjects, but through their policies and examples, they can create the pre-conditions that aid and abet the flourishing of religion.

Toward a Theology of Animals

> ⁷ And he issued a proclamation and published through Nineveh, "By the decree of the king and his nobles: Let neither man nor beast, herd nor flock, taste anything. Let them not feed or drink water, ⁸but let man and beast be covered with sackcloth, and let them call out mightily to God. Let everyone turn from his evil way and from the violence that is in his hands. ⁹ Who knows? God may turn and relent and turn from his fierce anger, so that we may not perish."

The king's decree includes animals (3:7). Even the beasts participate in the fast and put on sackcloth. In place of their saddles, harnesses, and reins, the animals will wear the clothes of penitence. It is funny to imagine these domestic and farm animals wearing sackcloth along with their masters, but there also is a serious theological point mentioned. Perhaps the king was doing more than he knew.

In the Bible, animals are always images or symbols of humanity. Different kinds of animals symbolize different kinds of people. Many Bible passages make these comparisons. In fact, the whole sacrificial system was predicated on the view that the animals were symbolic of humanity (especially the true human, Jesus Christ; Jn. 1:29). The lives of men and animals are always intertwined since animals share in the destiny of men. In Genesis 3, the curse that enters the world because of Adam's sin falls on the creation as a whole, including the animals. Because Adam sinned, now the animals will also suffer the effects of sin. But, if the curse includes animals, then redemption must include animals as well.

A prime example of this truth is that animals are saved from the Flood. God did not just save Noah and his family on the ark; He saved the animal kingdom as well. The meaning of Romans 8:17-25 is hotly debated, but there seems to be some intimation that the animals and the rest of the sub-human creation groan for the completion of our redemption as the children of God because, ultimately, they will be redeemed with us. They will live with us in the finalized new creation.

There are numerous mysteries and unanswerable questions, but at the very least, we can say that redemption is a package deal of cosmic proportions. Because of this connection of the lower creation with humanity, it is entirely appropriate to include the animals in this symbolic act of repentance. Thus, the king is not silly or ridiculous. His decree reflects the truths of Romans 8 a thousand years before Paul wrote Romans! Think about it: if Nineveh had been destroyed, not only would the human beings have suffered, but the animals too would have been destroyed. They were all in it together. The repentance of the people means the animals will be spared as well.

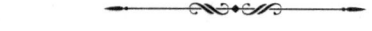

The King and the Captain

Chapter 3 raises a host of questions regarding God's repentance and the role of animals in redemption, but it also provides several connections and parallels between the ship captain in chapter 1 and the Ninevite king in chapter 3. The first chapter of this book has given us an example of Gentile repentance and conversion; now, we have another similar example. The repentance of the captain and the ship crew matches the repentance of the king and the city. The captain of the ship has his counterpart in the Ninevite king, just as the sailors have their counterpart in the citizens of the city. In 1:6, the captain says to Jonah, "Get up and pray to your God. Perhaps your God will consider us, so that we will not perish." In 3:9, the king uses almost identical language. He says,

"Who knows, perhaps God will relent and turn away from his fierce anger so that we will not perish." The two statements by the captain and the king echo one another.

More to the point, both speeches are theologically impeccable, even though the speakers are not trained in biblical theology as Jonah was. In each case, the leader does not presume upon God's mercy and God's sovereign freedom is acknowledged. That is to say, (to put it in our categories) both the captain and the king believe God is sovereign and free in the way He bestows mercy. God gives grace as He wills, when he wills, to whom He wills, and how He wills. There is no presumption on their part.

The essential question that they ask, "Who knows, perhaps God will show mercy and relent?" is a paraphrase of Joel 2:14. This assumption is the right thing to say when faced with impending disaster. Joel served as a prophet around the same time as Jonah. Israelites in Jonah's day reading this story probably would have known Joel's book as well. So when they heard this language, "Perhaps God will relent—who knows?" they would have heard the echo of one of their own prophets on the lips of these pagan leaders.

The captain and the king also acknowledge there is a ray of hope even in the most desperate circumstances. They suggest that through prayer and repentance, it is possible to avert the great calamities they face. In other words, they never give up or become fatalistic. They do not presume on God's grace, but they do not despair of God's grace either. As hopeless as their situations look, both men hope against hope in God's mercy. They cling to the truth that God is merciful.

This parallel between the ship in chapter 1 and the city in chapter 3 is a constant reminder to us that those who are willing to cling to God's mercy as their only hope in the face of judgment will find that the Lord does indeed rescue them. It is a simple lesson, but it is a lesson that no Christian will ever outgrow. We never get past our need for God's mercy.

Repentance and Covenant

¹⁰ When God saw what they did, how they turned from their evil way, God relented of the disaster that he had said he would do to them, and he did not do it.

We have now seen how Nineveh responded to God's decree of judgment and the identical connections between the king and the sailors. Now, in verse 10, God responds to the king's decree of repentance. Because the Ninevites repented of their evil, God repents of the judgment He was going to bring upon them. Their repentance, in effect, persuades God to change His course of action. If they had not repented—and we need to understand this and take the contingency seriously—God would not have either. If the Ninevites had faced the threat of destruction and decided to revel during their last forty days, their time would have expired and Nineveh would have ended up looking just like Sodom and Gomorrah. Nineveh would have been destroyed in forty days rather than several generations later, as was the case.

In some mysterious way, in a fashion that we will never be able to fathom fully, our repentance (or lack of it) affects God's response. Yes, God is fully sovereign, planning everything from the beginning to the end of history, not just the big things but the small details. But the Bible presents God as not only sovereign, ruling over all things, but also as intimately involved and responsive to things that are going on within His creation. There is no hint in the Bible that God's sovereignty cancels out or even limits human responsibility. There is no indication in the Bible that God's sovereign plan from eternity makes our prayers or our actions unnecessary or ineffective in any way whatsoever. We could say just the reverse: Because God's sovereign decree stands behind our prayers and our actions, we know they will be effective.

Strangely, God's plan includes our free actions. Not only that, but God's plan also includes God's response to those free actions on our part. That is the Biblical truth that we are faced with in Jonah 3 (and elsewhere). However, this is not an isolated incident where God changes his mind. In Exodus 32, Amos 7, and Jeremiah 18, God is more than willing to change what He will do in response to actions on the part of His creatures. In each of those cases, some action on the part of men, whether prayer or repentance, leads to a change in God's intentions. We dare not take the bulldozer of scholastic Calvinism and run over these texts because they are hard to package up into a neat and tidy theological system. Instead, we must affirm both God's sovereign decree and transcendence, as well as his active, responsive, immanent involvement in the creation.

What persuaded God to relent from his earlier intentions of judgment? What turned God from wrath to mercy? We may have an answer in a familiar case in Exodus 32. In that passage, God was going to destroy Israel and wipe her off the face of the earth. Instead, Moses stood up and prayed on behalf of the people, reminding God of the great promises that He has made. Moses reminds God that God's own reputation in the world is at stake in what happens with Israel. Jonah has no interest in being another Moses by interceding for Nineveh. The Ninevites are on their own as far as he is concerned. What do the Ninevites do that persuades God to change his mind? Verse 10 answers: "When God saw what they did, how they turned from their evil way, God relented of the disaster that he had said he would do to them, and he did not do it." God did not just hear their words; He saw their works. They backed up their profession of repentance with changed lives and adopted rituals of repentance among all the people. The Ninevites did not merely adopt new ideas or subscribe to a new set of doctrines. When God saw their changed deeds, specifically their turning from ways of violence to ways of love, He relented in His anger against them. Their repentance manifested itself socially. It was directed toward God since His threat prompted it. But it was most evident on the horizontal plane. They changed how they treated one another in the city by moving away from violent relationships to treating one another with kindness, tenderness, forgiveness, and love.

This is a wonderful model of biblical repentance. Repentance manifests itself not merely in words but actions. Biblically, to repent is to adopt a new way of life. The word *repent* means to turn around; it means the repentant one's life receives a whole new orientation, and a whole new direction. Nineveh shaped up in forty days. When God saw their works, He changed His mind as well. They changed the way they lived and so God changed His mind about them.

Throughout the Bible as a whole, on page after page, we find that salvation necessitates and includes a new obedient way of life. Those who are saved by God are those who repent and walk in faithfulness. Yes, we have to have the doctrines of grace and signs of the covenant in baptism and the Supper, but unless those things are backed up with lives of faithfulness, they will be hung around our necks as we are thrown into the deepest pits of Sheol. We must back up our professions of faith and participation in the sacraments with lives of obedience. Only the narrow way leads to salvation and only those who repent will escape the coming wrath.

This is the message of the prophets and John the Baptist and the entirety of Scriptures. The Ninevites believed God—as it says in verse 5. They believed the word that God spoke through the prophet Jonah. And, no doubt, they were justified by that faith, and by that faith alone. But that response of faith justified them and changed God's mind about them only because it was a living, obedient, and repentant faith. It was a faith that manifested itself in a changed way of life, as they turned from their evil and violent ways and practiced love and mercy.

We must always remember the covenant has two sides: promise and threat, blessing and judgment. The Ninevites got the threat side in Jonah's preaching because, after all, they were outside of the covenant altogether. But, because they believed, repented, and obeyed, they moved from the realm of covenant wrath into the realm of covenant blessing.

Those who place their trust in Yahweh are on the blessing side of the covenant. God promises everything to us, and so we should take great comfort in knowing that God is not angry with us, and has accepted us in Christ. We need to be reminded of those things so that we can continually rejoice in them. But we also need to know that God can change His mind about us, too. If we forsake God and His people, if we abandon the church catholic to worship idols, if we become hypocrites hiding a life of rebellion under a veneer of orthodoxy, God will turn His grace into fierce anger (cf. Jer. 18). Instead of pouring grace, He will pour out judgment. The good that God said He would bring upon us will turn to great calamity instead.

Israel learned that lesson soon enough. Israel was God's covenant people, in possession of the covenant blessings and heritage. When Jeremiah announced the coming judgment, the people pointed to the temple as proof that they were immune to God's wrath (Jer. 7). And yet, their presumptions proved false. Pagan armies came and carried Israel into exile, destroying the temple and leaving not one stone standing on another. God pulled no punches in hitting Israel with the curses of the covenant. In Christ, God bestows His grace upon us. But we must never become arrogant or boastful about it. We must never look down upon the unsaved, the Ninevites of our day, with a sense of superiority, thinking we are so much better than they are. We must not be like the Pharisee who prayed, "I thank God I'm not like other men." Instead, our prayer must be, "But for the grace of God, that would be me too." In Jonah, the Christian remembers that only the mercy of God is sufficient to save us.

4

Jonah's Last Stand

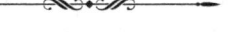

Jonah 4:1-11

By now, we are quite familiar with the basic meaning of the book of Jonah. Jonah was a prophet in northern Israel at a time when the nation was rebellious. Jonah knew what this meant: Israel would soon be judged for her stubborn waywardness. Jonah knew that sooner or later, all the curses of the covenant would come crashing down on their heads. He knew that sooner or later, Israel would be driven by a pagan nation out of the land of promise and into exile, and Jonah knew the most likely instrument for bringing about this exile was the nation of Assyria. After all, Assyria was the world's greatest empire, the lone superpower of the day. Indeed, Assyrian forces were already encroaching on Israel's turf, drawing ever closer to the land of the covenant people. They were already practically knocking on Israel's door.

Thus, the prophet receives God's command to go up to Nineveh, Jonah wants no part of it. Sure, God gave him a message of doom and disaster, but Jonah was familiar with God's mercy. He knows that if God is sending the Assyrians a prophet to minister his Word, it can only be because God has some deeper intention to bless this Gentile nation. This warning will be a means of grace. Jonah does not want to have anything to do with blessing Assyria. He wants Assyria destroyed because, at the very least, that might buy Israel a little more time for her to repent and avoid her own judgment.

But Jonah is like Midas, the famous king of Greek mythology: everything he touches turns to gold. Everyone he preaches to converts. He runs away on a boat to Tarshish, but when he finally has to tell these pagan sailors who he is and who he serves, they repent on the spot. And, of course, if Jonah's disobedience leads to salvation for this handful of sailors, how much more will his obedience lead to even greater salvation for the great Gentile empire of Nineveh (cf. Rom. 11)!

Jonah was thrown overboard into the sea by the sailors. He spent three days and nights in the belly of a fish. This was an acted-out prophecy, revealing what is to come in Israel's future. He symbolizes Israel, even as the fish symbolizes Assyria. Jonah's time spent in the belly of the fish corresponds to Israel's time in exile. But just as Jonah is resurrected on the third day and returns to dry land, so Israel will be resurrected out of exile and will return to her land. Just as Jonah came forth from the fish with a renewed call to fulfill his mission to the nations, so Israel will return from exile with a new call to fulfill her mission to the world.

Afterward, Jonah goes forth and preaches to Nineveh. The city hears this message that in forty days she will be overturned. Amazingly, the city responds to the threat of doom with genuine repentance. She turns from her evil to the Lord. God then responds to Nineveh's repentance by repenting Himself. He turns from the evil that He had in store for the city of Nineveh because He is pleased with the city's transformation.

But how does the prophet Jonah respond when he sees Nineveh's repentance? Does he see Nineveh as God sees her? Will he have the same kind of pity on her and forgive her for her sin? Or, will he harden his heart against Nineveh? In Jonah 4, we find that when Jonah sees their repentance, he becomes furious. He asks God, essentially: "How dare you show mercy to these international outlaws? How dare you share our blessing and our salvation with those who are outside Israel?" Jonah's response is the epitome of self-righteousness. When Jonah got rescued from the fish, he was so joyous he sang about it! He was delighted to find deliverance from his sin. But when God saves Nineveh from her danger, Jonah became so angry that he asked God to strike him dead. It is as though he says to the Lord, "You can forgive Nineveh over my dead body. That's the way I'd like it."

The question that flows out of Jonah 4 is plain: Whose attitude will we copy? Whose heart will we share? Will we be like God and see the world through the lenses of mercy and compassion? Or, will we be like Jonah, glad to have our salvation but content to let the world around us go to hell in a hand-basket?

Prophet vs. God

> [1] But it displeased Jonah exceedingly, and he was angry. [2] And he prayed to the Lord and said, "O Lord, is not this what I said when I was yet in my country? That is why I made haste to flee to Tarshish; for I knew that you are a gracious God and merciful, slow to anger and abounding in steadfast love, and relenting from disaster. [3] Therefore now, O Lord, please take my life from me, for it is better for me to die than to live." [4] And the Lord said, "Do you do well to be angry?"

Like the rest of the book, this chapter is a literary masterpiece. In this concluding chapter of the book, the author has outdone himself. These closing verses show forth true literary beauty and artistry, and we need to catch a glimpse of that. The forty-day time bomb that Jonah had planted in Nineveh turns out to be a dud. Everyone in the passage—the Ninevite citizens, the king of Nineveh, the animals in Nineveh, even God himself after a fashion—is repentant. But Jonah is resolutely unrepentant.

Verse 1 begins to set up a contrast between God and Jonah. It is much clearer in the Hebrew than in English, but it is there nonetheless. Look at the sequence of thought going back to chapter 3. In 3:9, the king says, "Perhaps God will turn from his fierce anger." Then, in 4:1, Jonah himself becomes angry. Right where God's anger ends, Jonah's anger begins. It is as though God puts out His fire right at the time when Jonah's fire of anger catches on. God is slow to anger. It would have taken Him a full 40 days to warm up into a full fury of wrath so that He could destroy the city of Nineveh. Then, when the people repent, His anger immediately subsides. But when Jonah sees that Nineveh has repented, he immediately gets angry.

There also is a play on the word *evil* in the story. The Hebrew word *evil* is a bit broader than our English term. The word is used three times in this context, which makes for a clever pun. The word *evil* in Hebrew could be used to describe moral evil, such as that which the Ninevites were committing, or the word could refer to some great disaster or calamity, such as the evil God said He would bring about against Nineveh. Finally, the Hebrew word for *evil* could suggest any kind of discomfort or pain, such as the evil that Jonah experiences after Nineveh has repented and God has relented in 4:1.

So this is how the text works: In 3:10, God saw they turned from their evil and relented from the evil that He said He would bring against them. How does Jonah respond? In 4:1, all this turns out to be a great evil to Jonah. It displeases him. It is evil to him that things turned out this way. Nineveh's turning from evil is itself an evil to Jonah. God's turning from the evil that He had planned is evil to Jonah. Jonah's view of things is entirely antithetical to God's. In fact, Jonah himself has become evil right at the very time when Nineveh has ceased being evil and when God has turned from his evil intentions toward Nineveh. Suddenly, the tables have turned. In chapter 4, Nineveh and God stand together, aligned against Jonah, the Jewish prophet. Nineveh is now on God's side in the grand scheme of things, and this Jewish prophet stands alone against Nineveh and God.

In verse 2, Jonah prays, but his prayer is hardly an act of piety. It is a self-centered prayer, if there ever was one. It rivals the prayer of the Pharisee in Luke 18 in the parable Jesus taught. Several details of the prayer show what is going on in Jonah's heart. First, he says, "Back when I was in my own country..." In other words, he regards Israel as his own people, rather than as God's country. He speaks of the nation as his own possession. More than that, he is choosing to ally himself with rebellious Israel rather than repentant Nineveh. His people are defined by ethnicity and blood, not by repentance and righteousness. Obviously, love for one's nation and family usually are virtues. Patriotism and family loyalty have their place. We are not indifferent to blood and soil because we are not Gnostics. This was especially true for ancient Israel since they were God's chosen family living in His holy land. But love for God takes precedence over all other loves. While we love people with whom we share blood and land, we must always have a higher loyalty to God's people, wherever they are found. Jonah's response to Ninevah's repentance exposed him as an idolater.

Secondly, Jonah goes on: "For I knew that you are a gracious God and merciful, slow to anger and abounding in steadfast love, and relenting from disaster." In these words, Jonah quotes several Old Testament texts about God's mercy and compassion. Taken together, this statement forms a virtual creedal statement of who God is in Old Testament language. These were the words God used to describe His glorious character in His supreme act of self-revelation in the old covenant (Exod. 34:6). This collection of divine attributes—graciousness, mercy, longsuffering, full of lovingkindness, and relenting from disaster—appear together again and again. This is simply who God is.

But it is precisely this description of God's character that draws Jonah's ire. Jonah's prayer is only prayer in a highly ironic sense. Jonah lists out these attributes, not so much because he wants to praise God for them; instead, it is almost as though Jonah is accusing God of these things. It is as though Jonah says, "I've got a case against you, Lord. My problem with you is that you're merciful, you show lovingkindness, and you are the God who relents. God, you love people I don't like! You have saved the wrong people—my enemies!"

Jonah speaks of the Lord's *lovingkindness*, the well-known Hebrew term *hesed*. It stands for God's covenant love or covenant kindness or covenant fidelity. What seems to aggravate Jonah is that these uncovenanted people in Nineveh have received God's covenanted mercy. God has done for them what He typically does for Israel. Does this sound familiar? Think about the Pharisees and other leading Jews and their reaction to the inclusion of the Gentiles after Jesus' death and resurrection.

Jonah knows the truth of Isaiah 28:21, namely, that judgment is God's strange work. God exercises a kind of holy reluctance when it comes to punishing people and pouring out wrath. God takes no pleasure in the death of the wicked (Ezek. 33:11). Jonah, however, would take great pleasure in the death of other wicked people. He would be delighted to see the Ninevites get hammered by God's club. But God does not feel this way. There is a clear contrast between God's attitude and Jonah's attitude. The narrative builds toward a showdown between the Lord and Israel's representative prophet.

What Jonah literally says in verse 2, is "Lord, was it not my word when I was still in my own country?" "My word" is the key. He is essentially saying, "Lord, my prophecy came true, but yours did not." "My word" is the same formula in Hebrew that God uses to speak of His own prophecies and declarations. God often speaks of "My word" as a way of describing His divine declaration. Jonah is setting his word—"my word"—over and against God's word.

This theme of confrontation of two "words," of Jonah versus the Lord, emerges as the main theme in chapter 4, as the dialogue between Jonah and God continues. Note these facts from the Hebrew text: Jonah's first speech in chapter 4 has thirty-nine words. God's last speech, which concludes the book, has thirty-nine words. God's question in verse 4 has three words. Jonah responds with a question of his own in verse 8, and it consists of three words. God says five words in verse 9, and Jonah responds in the same verse with five words of his own. Jonah matches his word against the Lord's word, word for word.

We are not necessarily arguing for counting words in passages of the Hebrew Bible. But when something like this happens, it is not a coincidence but a careful literary design. That is not to say it has been fabricated by the author of the book; after all, if God controls both the unfolding of history as well as the writing of Scripture, there is no reason why the actual interchange between the Lord and the prophet could not have taken precisely this shape. These speeches match and correspond with each other. Jonah sets his word up against God's word by saying that God has no right to show mercy to Nineveh. God, in turn, is saying that Jonah has no right to be angry with the way that He has shown mercy. He will have mercy on whom He will have mercy.

The prophet wants to go toe to toe with the Almighty God. He wants to challenge the very sovereignty of God in salvation. In one corner stands the self-righteous, angry prophet, and in the other corner stands the longsuffering, merciful God. While the prophet pleads for a suicidal showdown, the Lord pleads with the prophet to repent and be reconciled.

Mercy upon Mercy, Even to the Unmerciful!

The reader might think that by now God would be sick and tired of this self-pitying prophet. And yet we find that the Lord is still gracious to him. God is still patient with Jonah, even as He was patient with the Ninevites, even as He has been patient with Israel.

The Lord's mercy toward Nineveh does not make Him unmerciful toward Jonah. He cares for this one wayward, rebellious prophet, even as He cares for the Ninevite masses. Love for one people group does not exclude love for another. Look at God's incredible long-suffering in this passage. Twice in this context, Jonah says that he wants to die—in verse 3 and again in verse 8. It is almost like he is asking for a kind of divine euthanasia. He is not going to kill himself, but he wants God to do his dirty work for him. He has a death wish. He would rather die than see Assyria blessed. He would rather die than watch his beloved country get cursed.

This response is a typical human reaction to frustration. Most of us have probably felt like Jonah does here at one time or another. Most of us have probably had at least a time or two when we have been angry enough to die. We need to take stock of ourselves in these kinds of situations. If we do feel this way, if we would rather die than go on with the Lord, it is most likely a sign that at some level, our hearts are battling an idol. It means we are probably seeking meaning and significance in something other than God. And now that that thing is gone, or at least threatened, we are not sure whether we can go on living. In Jonah's case, that idol that gave life meaning was the nation of Israel itself, specifically Israel's exclusive status over and against the nations.

This passage has irony written all over it: here is Jonah, speaking to God, the One who gives life meaning and purpose, and Jonah is saying to God, "My life has no meaning or purpose. I want to die now that Israel, my people, have lost their special privileges." Sadly, this is an attitude that Israel carries down into the New Testament. We see it crop up in the Gospels, Galatians, Romans, and elsewhere. This attitude is all the more ironic because Israel only existed because of God's good pleasure. God's whole purpose in creating and calling the nation of Israel was so that she could, in turn, extend her blessings to the other nations. Once again, Jonah has it all backwards.

Think of the first explicit, full-fledged prophet in the Bible; the first man who is said to occupy the office of prophet is Abraham. Consider Abraham's actions, how he views the cities and nations of the world. Abraham has been set apart by God's covenant as the pioneer of the Jewish nation. But what does he do? Of all places, he seeks the good of Sodom and Gomorrah! He tries to persuade God to spare them. As one of God's counselors, he gives God good counsel, counsel that is consistent with God's character, with His mercy and His lovingkindness.

Many centuries later, Jonah enters the scene as an anti-Abraham figure. He wants the pagan city destroyed rather than saved. He would rather die himself than see Nineveh receive mercy. He does not care if there are ten righteous people in the city. He does not care if there are 100,000 righteous people in the city. He still wants it destroyed.

In the new covenant, we are all prophets (I Pet. 2:9). We are all given access to the throne of grace, where we serve as God's chief counselors. We should pray on behalf of the cities and nations of the world, that God might show them mercy. Like Abraham, and unlike Jonah, we should use our privileged prophetic position to intercede for outsiders, who are still strangers to God's mercy and stand under the threat of condemnation. To do otherwise is to make prayer self-serving and is to work at cross purposes with God Himself.

Feasting Alone

> [5] Jonah went out of the city and sat to the east of the city and made a booth for himself there. He sat under it in the shade, till he should see what would become of the city.

In verse 5, as Jonah realizes what is going on, he goes out east of the city. Of course, east is the direction men go when they are sent away from the presence of God. Think of Cain dwelling east of Eden, sent away from the face of God. Or, visualize the tabernacle: entrance into God's presence was made by traveling back westward, passing through the cherubim-stitched curtains, into the Holy Place and the Holy of Holies. Jonah goes out to the east of the city, and there he sits down. He has placed himself outside the sphere of blessing. Nineveh has become a new Jerusalem—a new embodiment of the city of God—but Jonah is excluded because of his self-righteousness and pride. He is already beginning to taste the curse God has in store for the nation of Israel.

Note that Jonah sits down. But unlike the Ninevite king in chapter 3, who sat in dust and ashes and repented, Jonah sits down in unrepentance and hardness of heart. The Ninevites have become law-keepers, putting Jonah to shame. Paul develops a similar argument against unbelieving Israel in Romans 2 when he observes that there are Gentiles who do not have the law by nature (birth/culture), but who do the things of the law—and thus they put to shame the Jews who possess the law by nature but do not do what it says.

Then, in verse 5 we are told that Jonah makes a shelter, a sort of miniature tabernacle, for himself. The word used for this little hut is the same word used for the small structures ("tabernacles") built during the Feast of Booths (or, the Feast of Tabernacles or Feast of Ingathering; see Zech. 14). So, again, there is a great deal of irony at work, all at Jonah's expense. The Feast of Tabernacles was one of Israel's major feasts. For seven days the people camped out in Jerusalem in little tree houses. These shelters were replicas of God's house, the tabernacle/temple. Of course, this was a sign that their dwelling was with God. Moreover, it pointed ahead to the future when they would dwell in the tabernacle, through their final High Priest, Jesus Christ (cf. John 1:14).

But this feast was also an eschatological sign in another way. It came at the end of the Israelite year and symbolized the nations being drawn into God's kingdom. Gentiles could participate in this feast along with Jews. At this feast, seventy bulls were sacrificed in seven days, obviously representing the seventy nations of the world, going back to the table of nations in Genesis 10.

But something is not quite right in Jonah 4. Jonah is, as it were, having his own little feast of tabernacles, but it is a perverted version of the feast. It is as if he were having communion in private, with no one else around to commune. Jonah's "tabernacle" is a distortion of the Feast of Tabernacles. There are no Gentiles gathered in with him! He does not even want the Gentiles to be gathered into God's kingdom. In fact, in light of the parable of the prodigal son in Luke 15, we could say Jonah resembles the older brother of the Old Testament. He does not want to celebrate the salvation or repentance of someone else. He would rather be alone than celebrate another's turning to God. He is not like the angels in heaven who rejoice over the repentance of even one sinner (Luke 15:10). In some ways, Jonah is the anti-angelic prophet.

We can come at this from another angle as well. The whole scene represents the problem with Israel. These miniature tabernacles that the Israelites would build during the Feast of Tabernacles symbolize the tabernacle or the temple, as we have already noted. Jonah is enjoying his little tabernacle all by himself. But in a sense, that is symbolic of what Israel was doing with the temple in Jerusalem. Rather than using the temple in Jerusalem as a house of prayer for all nations (Isa. 56:7), Israel used the temple in reverse fashion, a perversion of its true purpose. She pushed the nations even farther away from the temple, trying to keep the temple, and therefore the presence of God, all to herself. Jonah's sin is Israel's sin, the sin of seeking to hoard and monopolize God's gifts.

The Trickster God

> ⁶ Now the Lord God appointed a plant and made it come up over Jonah, that it might be a shade over his head, to save him from his discomfort. So Jonah was exceedingly glad because of the plant. ⁷ But when dawn came up the next day, God appointed a worm that attacked the plant, so that it withered. ⁸ When the sun rose, God appointed a scorching east wind, and the sun beat down on the head of Jonah so that he was faint. And he asked that he might die and said, "It is better for me to die than to live."

In verses 6-8, God plays a little trick on Jonah to teach him a lesson. God provides a shade plant that grows overnight, much to Jonah's delight. The plant grows up rapidly to protect the prophet. But the next day, God provides a worm to destroy it.

The whole episode once again demonstrates God's sovereignty over His creation. It is another symbolically enacted parable, pointing to Israel's future: the plant (like the fish) represents Assyria. God will preserve His people, even as He chastens them. Despite what Jonah thinks, his preaching to Nineveh will ultimately benefit Israel because these God-fearers will break Israel's fall when they are scattered among the nations. Jonah's ministry will "soften up" Assyria so that when they usher Israel into exile, it will not be as bad as it would have otherwise been. God will shelter His people in exile.

The worm represents the serpent, that is, Satan (cf. Gen. 3). Nineveh will eventually apostatize and perish (cf. Nahum), no longer shielding Israel from God's wrath (represented by the sun and wind). Thus, Israel better shape up while there is still time. The sun "attacks" Jonah even as the worm "attacked" the plant. In other words, Israel is in grave danger. Jonah is in the same "misery" (4:6) as Nineveh (1:2). The fact that the same word is used of Jonah's plight and Nineveh's plight shows that Israel needs God's grace and rescue every bit as much as the pagans. Israel is no better than the nations. How dare she look down on them in pride!

God is giving Jonah the big picture through these symbols. Judgment (exile) will come, but Israel will still have an opportunity to repent. Assyria will provide shelter for a time, but Israel must learn the lesson of the fish and the plant lest she perish too. We must learn that God's chastening hand may hurt, but it also provides an opportunity to repent.

Jonah is mad that his plant is taken away the next day, which means he has not grasped what he has affirmed in 2:9 when he declares that salvation is of the LORD. Jonah pitied the plant because it served his interests and provided for his comfort. And that brings us to the final dialogue between Jonah and God in verses 9-11.

The Final Word

⁹ But God said to Jonah, "Do you do well to be angry for the plant?" And he said, "Yes, I do well to be angry, angry enough to die." ¹⁰ And the Lord said, "You pity the plant, for which you did not labor, nor did you make it grow, which came into being in a night and perished in a night. ¹¹ And should not I pity Nineveh, that great city, in which there are more than 120,000 persons who do not know their right hand from their left, and also much cattle?

In verse 9, God points out to Jonah that he had pity on the plant, a plant which he had not worked for, which he had not made to grow. Yet, by contrast, Jonah does not pity the people of Nineveh and her animals. The logic here is obvious: people are more important than plants because people are made in God's image. Even animals are more important than plants in terms of the hierarchy of things. How can Jonah fail to pity the people of Nineveh while pitying a plant that has been destroyed? But Jonah has no regard for the more than 120,000 inhabitants of Nineveh.

Why does God bring in the population of the city in the book's closing verse? Archaeologically, we are not certain how many people lived in Nineveh at this time, though it probably was the world's largest city at that point. It could very well have had a whole lot more than 120,000 people in it. This number may refer to the number of households or the number of very young children in the city. Whatever the case, the number is symbolic: 120,000 is 12 x 10,000. In other words, it is the number of the tribes of Israel multiplied by 10,000.

Is Nineveh being presented as something of a new Israel, even an enlarged Israel (cf. Rev. 7)? At the very least, we can say that Nineveh is being presented as something of a shadow of Israel.

In a sense, the Ninevites have become true Israelites, even apart from having the law or even apart from being circumcised (cf. Rom. 2). Because of their repentance and faith, they have become Spiritual Jews. Once again, this is eschatological foreshadowing, pointing to the creation of a new Israel in the new covenant era. This new Israel will include the Gentiles in fullness (cf. Gal. 6:16).

The Sum of the Matter: Saved to Serve

The end of the book brings us back to where we started. Indeed, we have come full circle as far as Jonah is concerned. The book ends just as it began for God as well. The book started with God's word of compassion for the great city of Nineveh, and it ends with God proclaiming His compassion for the city. God says He is full of mercy toward the people of Nineveh because they are miserable, helpless, and ignorant. They do not even know their right hand from their left, theologically or morally speaking. These people are in a wretched, miserable condition, but God takes care of them. The narrative is enveloped by God's mercy from beginning to end.

God has the first and last word in this book, and yet the final word comes in the form of a question, one that is posed not only to Jonah but to all of us. And it is a question that we will answer in the way that we live our lives. This question becomes the overriding message of the book. If it sounds like the application has already been noted in several previous chapters, that is by design. Martin Luther said that he was so fixated on the doctrine of justification that he was playing a one-stringed harp. But he played it magnificently! In a way, Jonah is a one-stringed harp— only, in this case, that one string is compassion, particularly divine compassion as a model and motive for the compassion of God's people. The writer of Jonah is a one-stringed story-teller because every chapter comes back to this same theme.

The question that God poses to Jonah, and therefore to us, is this: Will you have a heart for the world? Will you live a life of compassion and tenderness and winsomeness and kindness? Or, will you be bitter and jealous and self-righteous? These are questions that need answering. These are questions that we will each answer in one way or another through the whole course of our lives. We are continually moving in one of these two directions by the way we live and speak. Are we seeking to spread the good news of God's compassion to the world in Christ, or are we too self-absorbed and self-righteous to help anyone else? The book of Jonah calls us to be a compassionate people. Compassion does not cancel out the need for repentance. It does not make us moral relativists unable to speak the truth. Sometimes compassion will be offensive because compassion compels us to tell sinners the truth about their sin. But if we are genuinely compassionate, we will seek to carry forward the mission God has given to us of discipling the nations.

Jonah reminds us that God saves us so that we might serve. God works in us so that He might work through us. We need to see that our own personal salvation is part of something much greater that God is accomplishing in His creation. God has a project to save the entire world, to bless all the families of the earth, and we are part of that project.

In J. R. R. Tolkien's classic work, *The Hobbit*, which is the prelude to *The Lord of the Rings* trilogy, Bilbo Baggins (a hobbit) has been spared in one great adventure after another on his way to recover a lost treasure with some dwarves. The dwarves' ancestral treasure had been taken captive by a dragon and Bilbo was recruited to help. Bilbo was rather reluctant to join the mission but ends up playing a vital role. After they have succeeded (with quite a bit of help from others), Bilbo journeys back home with his little share of the treasure. Sometime later, the wise wizard Gandalf comes to visit Bilbo. As Bilbo hears of the great prosperity that has overtaken the land after the killing of the dragon, he exclaims, "Then the old prophecies and songs have turned out to be true, after a fashion!" Gandalf replies, "Of course! And why shouldn't they? Surely you don't disbelieve the prophecies, because you had a hand in bringing them about yourself? You don't really suppose that all your adventures and escapes were managed by mere luck, just for your sole benefit?"

Gandalf reminds Bilbo that his role in the story is only a chapter in a larger, longer narrative. His role is an essential part of the story, to be sure, but a Greater Power is at work behind the scenes. Like Bilbo, if we are faithful to the vocation God gives us, we may be surprised to find glorious prophecies coming true right before our eyes! God will slay dragons and establish peace and the peoples of the earth will be drawn into the kingdom and Jesus will take possession of the nations as His promised inheritance. God has promised a magnificent future for the world, but it only comes to pass as His people play their part by living sacrificially on behalf of others.

Gandalf then goes on to say, "You are a very fine person, Mr. Baggins, and I am very fond of you but you are only quite a little fellow in a wide world after all." Bilbo is quickly given proper perspective. He hands Gandalf the tobacco jar and says, "Thank goodness!"

The same truth that Gandalf explained to Bilbo applies to Jonah and us. Jonah was quite a little fellow as well. Like Bilbo, we have a role to play, but we must not think of ourselves as irreplaceable. We will have a hand in the fulfillment of the prophecies of glory, but only because God promises to use our efforts.

All of Jonah's adventures—the storm at sea, getting thrown overboard, his escape from the fish on the third day, the shade plant that God provided for him—all these things happened, not for his sole benefit, but for the benefit of others. God had the whole wide world in view. It was for the good of the Assyrian empire, it was for the good of Israel, and it was for the good of the nations.

In the same way, God has saved us, not just for our sole, private benefit, but so that we can play our part in God's salvation of the wider world as well. All our adventures, all the twists and turns God brings us through, all the lessons He teaches us, all the suffering He brings us through, all the pains and frustrations, and all the deliverances he provides for us are part of His larger plan. These things do not happen merely for our own good (though that is true, per Rom. 8:28); they happen so that we can be of service to others. Whatever God has taught you, whatever ways He has blessed you, whatever victories He has given you, whatever comfort He has brought you—we are to use all of these things to benefit others. In this way, we come to share in God's compassionate mission toward the world. We bring the prophecies to pass and enter into everlasting joy.

The Unfinished Story

Jonah is a drama in two acts, with two scenes in each act. Thus, there are four scenes total that match up with the four chapters of the book. In the first scene, God says to Jonah, "Go to Nineveh" but Jonah runs in the opposite direction. He gets on a ship headed in the opposite way, to Tarshish. But a storm comes and as a result, Jonah ends up getting thrown overboard by reluctant Gentile sailors. The sailors convert when they hear who Jonah is and of the God he serves.

In the second scene, then, Jonah is swallowed up by a great fish. He remains in the belly of the fish three days and nights. God spares him, and so he praises God in a psalm of thanksgiving.

Then we come to scene three, which looks a whole lot like scene one. Once again, God comes to Jonah and tells him to go to Nineveh, which Jonah obeys. And so he goes to Nineveh where he preaches the message God has given to him. As a result, the Ninevites are saved, just as the sailors had been saved. In scenes one and three, a word from Jonah converts Gentiles.

Scene four matches up with chapter 4 of the book. Jonah goes outside the city. But instead of praising God for His work of salvation, we find that Jonah is grumbling angrily. It is the antithesis of scene two. He praises God for his own salvation, but shakes his fist in God's face when others are saved. This scene parallels chapter 2—Jonah prays inside the fish and outside the city—but also shows us that Jonah has not really changed his ways.

The first and the third scenes in the book both focus on the commission that God gives to Jonah to go and preach to Nineveh. The first time he disobeys, the second time he obeys. Scenes two and four form a pair. They deal with Jonah's response to God's salvation. In chapter 2, the second scene, Jonah rejoices in the fact that he has been saved, but at the end of the book, in the final scene, Jonah is angry that the Ninevites have been saved. This is the symmetry of the plot.

The purpose of the book, as we have seen again and again, is very plain. It shows us that the grace and the mercy of God are far deeper and far wider than we imagine. The purpose of the book is to show us that God loves the world. Like Jonah, we are called to be ambassadors of God's mercy and love. We are to carry forth His mercy into the world with our lips and our lives. We are to share God's heart for the world.

But while the book of Jonah has this simple symmetry, by the end, we find ourselves right back where we were at the beginning. The difference is that the book ends without really ending. It has an open-ended plot. Jonah began with the prophet in disobedience because he did not want to take God's grace to the Ninevites, and it ends with Jonah in disobedience because God has, in fact, given His grace and His salvation to the Ninevites. There is symmetry, but it is a symmetry of sinfulness. The question here, as with an unfinished story, is what happens next?

The Unfinished Mission of the Church

Jonah ends, and yet it leaves us unsatisfied. The story ends without ending, or at least it ends without a happy resolution. It ends with God asking Jonah a question that amounts to this: "Jonah, will you join me in having a heart for the world, and embracing a heart of compassion toward others?" We are not told how Jonah answered this question. The whole story of Jonah would have been a lot more cut and dry if it had ended at the conclusion of chapter 3. Instead, it keeps going and now we are left with this pressing question on our hands. We are left wondering if this story is a comedy or a tragedy. Jonah likely penned this book as a testament to his repentance, and if so, the question is now being posed to the people of God more broadly: "Will you see the compassion of God in your own life and extend it to others, even your enemies?"

The unanswered question at the end of the book calls us to consider whether we too—like the prophet—struggle to grasp this basic lesson about God's love and God's grace. The open-ended story allows us to write the ending of this story with our eyes. This story was written for the church and so God's people must finish it.

Earlier in the book, Jonah spent three days and three nights in the belly of the fish. Now, there is another three day/night pattern sequence at the end of the book, only this time, the prophet is outside the city. The reader needs to make this connection. In 3:4, Jonah makes his day-long journey through the city. He then goes outside the city and at 4:5, he builds a little booth to sleep. Overnight God causes a plant to grow up, and Jonah's second day is one of joy. He has shelter under the shade of the plant which God has provided. But on that second night, the plant perishes, and Jonah's third day is one of anguish as he suffers under the hot sun without any protection. But the book ends before we get to the third night. We are not told if Jonah overcame his anger, if he repented, and we are not told how he spent that third night. Again, that is the point: We are left asking and wondering, how will that third night go? But the question is not just, what will Jonah do next? The question is, what will I do next?

When Jonah came forth from the fish after the third night, he sang this song of praise back in Jonah 2. What is going to happen on this third night in Jonah 4? As the reader/hearer, you are now Jonah. You are put in his position. Thu, how will you spend that third night? How will you respond to God's mercy? The point is plain, and the call is clear—this is how God is stirring us to action.

God calls us to be tender, to be kind-hearted, to be loving, to be hospitable, to be compassionate. The book of Jonah compels us to share in God's love for the world, a love that knows no distinctions or bounds of nation or race. The only distinguishing feature that sets us apart is the fact that God has shown mercy to us. Will you show this mercy and compassion to others?

Appendix A

Jonah as a Biography of Human Maturation

The Book of Jonah is theologically rich in its assertions regarding God's sovereignty and particular ways in which God deals with humans in their rebellious and obedient stages of life. The full effect of a theological analysis of the book also provides a biographical outline for human behavior, especially as it pertains to human maturation.

While other books of the Bible may provide healthy glimpses into a full-orbed summary of maturation, Jonah uniquely positions itself to offer an overview in only 48 verses.

Taken as a whole, we propose that the book offers a holistic vision of the complexity of human growth as an image-bearer. In other words, the story of the prophet is a model for our Christian existence and our struggle to conform our lives to Messiah Jesus (Rom. 8:29). In this sense, Jonah is a precursor to the Pauline emphasis on warring against the flesh and the apostle's existential predicament in considering his disposition toward the good while contradicting that good at other times (Rom. 7:14-20).

Using the standard chapter division, it seems the Book of Jonah argues for four particular stages of Christian living, and they are a) the call to obedience, b) the response of grace, c) the rituals of sanctification, and d) the taste of mercy.

The Call to Obedience

The Christian life begins with a call to obedience. The call of Jonah in chapter one is a call to live out his prophetic calling. The post-Ascension saint receives a similar imperative, represented by the call placed on his head in baptism (Matt. 28:18-20). Every Christian is called to serve God and man, and to disciple the nations. We may even boldly say that no baptized Christian is exempt from the call of God. While Jonah had a distinct calling to the Gentiles, we too embrace that calling within our sphere of influence. The Christian bears the name of Christ and carries his calling wherever he is. Jonah's initial response took him on a downward path that led him eventually down to Sheol itself.

We know that God demands our obedience, but our natures fight the things we know to be true. Paul says that our nature wants to do the right thing, but it is in constant war against itself. The first affirmation of the Christian walk is that we are in an ongoing war against sin. Minimizing our own sins would be a peril to our growth in Christ. While Jonah's first response is one of consequential damage to the prophet, it is not far at all from our daily assumptions that we too can live in hidden harmony with ourselves apart from obedience to God's call. The response to such self-deception is to work daily at creating environments where sin is part of our daily conversation. Christians need other Christians in our war against sin.

Too often, those most reticent about confessing and thinking through the implications of their sins are also the ones who learn to dichotomize their lives into what they do in public and what they do in private. But the consequences of the Jonah story serve as an archetype for our own lives. God calls us to holistic obedience, and we must acknowledge that obedience is the way to

Appendix A

true life in the sight of God and man. Sin cannot be neatly divided. Sanctification is a call to growth, and the call to growth is a call to grasping the seriousness of disobedience in our lives.

Pastorally, those most secretive about their sins are the most prone to deep internal struggles about the Christian life. Unfortunately, sometimes we treat sin as such a private matter that we act as though confession is unnecessary. But the call to obedience is implicitly a call to understand our deep struggles with lust, gossip, immorality, and spiritual weariness. We must immerse ourselves in the knowledge of God's calling. Simply put, Christians are called to awareness of our tendency to war against the good.

We can master our external appearance to the detriment of our private appearance before God. The call to obedience is a call to acknowledge, which puts us in a constant sense of confusion with our own desire for righteousness, and simultaneously our soul and body's war against that righteousness. This complexity experienced by many in the Bible and throughout Church history should instruct us in our daily walk. God is constantly looking at our inward appearance, but we have often trained ourselves into a different language of acceptability by teaching ourselves and our children that warring against sin is merely an outward pursuit.

But the Jonah trajectory demands wrestling with the righteousness of confession by seeing sin for what it is while avoiding the temptations of introspectionism. The Christian objectively pursues goodness through the blessings of community and the fatherly absolution of the Triune God.

Jonah wrestles deeply with this, and by the end of chapter one, he delves into the abyss of his own sinfulness and prodigality. And from the depths of his transgressions, Jonah produces a song of praise.

The Response of Grace

Jonah's response in chapter two reveals the natural response of grace. He responds to his sin like a Christian, not in arrogance. He formulates prayers that are specific to his condition and aim directly at the heart of his disobedience. He refuses generic prayers hoping that something sticks in the walls of heaven. Instead, he takes psalms and strings them together in beauty and splendor because Jonah knows that only God's word can penetrate his heart. His emotional response to sin is flawed throughout, but the Word of the Lord is rich in describing sinfulness with precision.

Jonah says that everything dear to him means nothing if he does not engage his sin correctly. The Christian responds to grace by pouring our specific sins on him who took our sins and who rose victorious over sin (I Pet. 2:24). Jonah understands that the life of the covenant is a life in deep communion with God in response to his grace. Every act of disobedience presents a noble offer of grace, which takes us back to the place of God's dwelling (Jonah 2:4).

If the Christian life serves as an ambassador for sin, it is practically functioning as a rejection of the Christian walk. The Christian sees his sin and finds the most immediate path toward renewal. He engages the God who took him to the depths of the earth as the same God who can bring him to resurrection in his Christian life.

Jonah chooses the refuge of the psalms in the depths of the creature. The Christian response to grace must always be psalmically shaped. It must learn to interpret the pain of sin rightly and must also seek to develop a strategy for future living in the sight of God. For Jonah, there was no environment too foreign to human existence outside the ability to compose a new song unto the Lord.

Appendix A

The Rituals of Repentance

While Jonah seeks God's favor in this rich psalm, yet another aspect of the human grappling with sin comes into focus. This element is enshrined in the kingly response in the third chapter. We often expect godly responses from the veteran righteous saint, but at times, as in Jonah, it is the zeal of the newly transformed heart that offers a pure and ritualistically rich impulse to respond to God in particular ways. The third chapter of Jonah implies that true confession must create a culture of rituals that the Christian engages daily to demonstrate his allegiance to the God of heaven and earth.

In Jonah 3, the king of Nineveh embraces several rituals of repentance. He understands that God operates most clearly amid our habits. So the Ninevites believe, but the transformation from unholy to holy practices seals the favor of God. The text says that God saw what they did and relented, thus removing His judgment upon them.

The path to Christian growth is to embrace and form rituals that shape your response in times of uncertainty, in times of pain, and in times of new beginnings. No Christian society and no individual Christian can grasp the nature of sanctification without establishing rituals for growth. Indeed, one cannot pursue obedience rightly without establishing rituals. Too often, we want to jump into obedience by activistic endeavors in politics and culture. Still, the Christian life must be grounded in rituals of grace like indwelling the Bible, singing God's truth, faithful living in the assembly, good reading, showing hospitality, or whatever it may be. Every time we go through a crisis of thought, word, or deed, we must not abandon rituals because if we do, we forsake the very thing that returns us back to a life of peace and forgiveness. When we face challenges and undergo trials, we should cling more to our friendships, we should become closer to our church (as Jonah prayed), and we must pour even more of ourselves into developing the habits of grace.

Luther once argued that when the Christian is bombarded by the evil one, he urges the sufferer to "seek convivial company... dine, dance, joke, and sing."[15] The baptized man cannot allow evil to form his habits. Instead, the Christian's rituals are developed in a community of grace that will enable him to war against evil.

In Jonah, God spoke most clearly amid the rituals of repentance in Nineveh. When the king urged them to change their practices, the people changed their practices. So the greater King of glory calls His people to submit to rituals unto life, and He has promised that He will act with mercy in response to those practices.

The Taste of Mercy

The cycle of the Christian's journey to maturity still demands one more stage. It is the repetitive sequence of the psalmist (Ps. 136) and one which Jonah knew intellectually (Jonah 4:2) but struggled to experience personally in the last chapter. The Christian must experience the *hesed* of God. However, new mercies do not flow to the Christian who lives in opposition to mercy. New mercies come to those who desire to taste God's mercy and who wait upon God to do something beautiful out of ashes, something divine out of the mundane, something glorious out of the tragic.

There is no such thing as a Christian who lives in constant despair. If there is, the Gospel is a lie. The Christian must, at some point despite all the pain and persecution, taste that the Lord is good. He must realize that intellectual knowledge must translate into experiential knowledge. When God meets His people in the Scriptures, He turns their mourning into dancing. The consistent

---

15   Roland H. Bainton, *Here I Stand: A Life of Martin Luther* (New York: Abingdon Press, 1950), 285.

appeal of our age is to treat human happiness as the ultimate goal; thus, individuals will do whatever it takes to achieve such happiness through bodily transformation, as we see in the transgender community. But the satisfaction of knowing God's mercy is the only way to happiness and pleasure.

In chapter four, Jonah fails to see the goodness of God by letting his anger control his mind. He knows that God is merciful and slow to anger, but Jonah submits to the god of anger who takes captives gladly. He even says twice that he is angry enough to die. So, how does God respond to Jonah's anger? Instead of scolding His son and servant, God shows him just how far His mercy will go to take him from anger to satisfaction, from glory to glory, from uncertainty to protection. So, likewise, the Christian must taste the mercy of God and must be able to experience what that mercy looks like, tastes like, and sounds like.

And if that is not the case, there is a high degree of chance that there are step(s) in this outline of human sanctification absent in one's life, which necessarily derails the Christian's walk with God. If we overlook the importance of rituals or the nature of confession, if we think too highly of ourselves, we will be left with a truncated Gospel that makes us constantly doubt the goodness and compassion of God.

The Silence of the Journey

Jonah's reflection of his own journey ends with God's question. The beginning belongs to God and the end belongs to God. The human experience does not end with our unending inquisition of God's ways. At some point, God ends the conversation, which poses the inevitable question of allegiance. At some point, God's words come to an end, and the Christian must act on what he knows to be true about God.

The lack of an answer from Jonah at the end of the book is intentional, especially if we believe he penned this book. When the Bible speaks of the exile of God's people, amid confusion about who will rule over them and whether they will remain in exile forever, the Bible leaves the reader wondering. What will happen next? Will God's people remain in this darkness forever? And in every unanswered question, the implication is always the same: that the God who asks also answers the question with acts of grace on behalf of His own. Jonah did not need to speak, for he knew that God's purposes would prevail and that he would see the beauty of God's acts in his story. Prophets function as council members in God's courts. Jonah's context indicates that he knew the actions of God would prevail; therefore. His response must be one of total submission to the divine plan.

When we are left speechless at the end of this cycle of sin, confession, rituals and mercy, when we experience these things and eagerly pursue our growth and conformity to Christ, then we simply sit, as Jonah did, and acknowledge that God's means for our growth is often a long journey where sin is not hidden, where responding to grace is our sacred duty, where rituals of sanctification are observed, and where we taste God's mercies together. Through it all, God is there as He was with Jonah. He is also there, interceding for us in His glorified humanity, sympathizing with our weakness and raising us up to the heavenly places to taste and see His compassion and mercy.

Jonah is the archetype for sanctification because, in the end, we are all very much like him: eager to run away from our calling, wrestling with our identity, offering prayers to God in the depths of woes, and engaging the habits of grace. Jonah is each of us. We are Jonah. And only in Christ, the greater Jonah, who conquered Sheol and proclaimed victory to the captives, can we taste and see that He is good and that His mercies endure forever.

Appendix B

Does God Change His Mind?
A Complex Providence

God is absolutely sovereign. According to Scriptures, God has an eternal plan that encompasses everything that happens within his creation. Nothing can happen without God's knowledge because nothing happens apart from God's determination. Therefore, God's plan is dependent upon nothing because that plan already includes everything. Scripture repeatedly emphasizes this truth. In Daniel 4, Nebuchadnezzar confesses:

"God's dominion is an everlasting dominion, and His kingdom is from generation to generation. All the inhabitants of the earth are reputed to be nothing; He does according to his will in the army of heaven and among the inhabitants of the earth. No one can restrain His hand or say to Him, 'What have you done?'"

God controls the course of history. He can never be acted on from the outside against His will. In Lamentations, we read, "Who can speak and have it happen if the Lord has not decreed it. Is it not from the mouth of the Most High that both calamities and good things come?" Here we find that both good events and disasters are a part of God's eternal plan. Proverbs 16 points to God's sovereignty over human action: "A man's heart plans his way, but the Lord directs his steps." Whatever men do, they are under God's constant control and direction. Even the wicked actions of men and Satan are under God's control. In Acts 2, Peter preaches to those who crucified Jesus (undoubtedly the greatest criminal act ever!) that they "only did what God's hand and purpose had determined before should be done." Romans 8:28 uses this truth of God's total control to comfort us. Because God is sovereign and is never caught by surprise, we can know that He is working all things together for the good of His people. Our pain fits into his good and perfect plan, even if we cannot see how right now. Ephesians 1 situates our salvation within God's wider program for the creation and history. Election in Christ and predestination unto salvation are ways in which, as Paul says, "God works all things out according to His good pleasure and His eternal purpose." God determined beforehand whom He would save from the fallen human race so that nothing is left to chance. Everything hinges on God's will; nothing is left to the autonomy of the creature.

Throughout Scripture, we have clear examples of prophecies in which God reveals His plans for the future. God announces what He will do and then He does it. He has planned the future so He can reveal what is yet to come. God knows the past, present, and future because He planned the history of creation from beginning to end. He governs everything in heaven and earth, from the largest galaxy to the smallest subatomic particle. Because God has planned and controls all things, He never has to change His mind. God has planned from all eternity what He would do in space and time.

In 1 Samuel 15, Samuel declares, "God is not a man that He should repent." God is not like us. Many of us are inconsistent and indecisive, constantly second-guessing ourselves. Many of us change our minds all the time. God does not have a plan B and never has to make mid-course corrections. He never gets new information that makes Him rethink or alter His plans. He is unchanging. Every section of the Bible emphasizes this truth in one way or another. From the Pentateuch in Numbers 23: "God is not a man that He should change His mind or that He should repent." From the Psalter, in Psalm 33: "The council of the Lord stands forever, the plans of His heart to all generations." From the prophets, in Malachi 3: "I the Lord do not change." From the New Testament, in James 1: "God does not change like shifting shadows."

Many of us probably remember the initial time that we encountered these truths and how they overwhelmed us. We may not have liked these things at first, but in the end, we came to see that God's sovereignty is indisputably taught in the Scriptures and is, in fact, a source of great confidence and joy. God rules and controls all things with infinite power and wisdom. He has a fixed and unalterable plan and His will cannot be overturned. Whatever He has decreed, He performs. John Calvin sums it up well when he says, "God so attends to the regulation of individual events and they all proceed from His set plan that nothing takes place by chance."[16] The Westminster Confession teaches the same truth: "God, from all eternity did, by the most wise and holy counsel of His own will, freely and unchangeably ordained whatsoever comes to pass."

But in the Bible, we find another set of passages that seem to be in tension with the ones just mentioned. In Jonah 3, when the Ninevites repent, God also repents. This text appears to be just as straightforward as the others we have considered. God saw their works as they turned from their evil way to practice love and obedience, and He relented (or repented). In other words, God changed His mind. The Ninevites changed their minds and their course of action, and so God changed His mind and His course of action as well. Earlier in 1 Samuel 15, Samuel says that God is not a man that He should repent, but in the very same chapter, God rejects Saul as king. He changes His mind about Saul. He even says that He regrets making Saul king. Now, how can a sovereign God have regrets? How can the one who plans and controls all things change His mind?

We find other examples like this in Scripture. In the book of Exodus, God wants to destroy Israel because of her idolatry. But Moses stands in the gap and prays for the people, persuading

---

16 John Calvin, *Institutes of the Christian Religion*, I.16-18

God to change His mind, to turn away from judgment and hold off in pouring out His wrath upon the people. The prophet Amos does the same in chapter 7 of his prophecy. God gives the prophet a vision of how Israel will be destroyed. The prophet prays for God to relent and God does so. God changes His mind, turning from wrath against Israel to mercy. Judging from these passages in Exodus and Amos, we might even say it looks like God can be talked out of things pretty easily! God's plans can indeed change because of our prayers and actions.

So how do we fit all this together? The truth is most Christians have a tough time doing so. There are those Christians who emphasize the first batch of passages that we looked at, which emphasize God's sovereignty. Christians who fall into this category tend to be confident and secure in the face of trials and adversity because they know that all these things are still in God's plan. But very often, these Christians view God as distant and even aloof. They know that God is the transcendent Lord, but He seems uninvolved in their day-to-day affairs. As a result, prayer (that is, intimate conversation with God) suffers. After all, God already knows, so why pray? Why act to do something if God has already predestined everything? Sometimes these Christians have come to be known as the "frozen chosen" (a hard-earned nickname, no doubt!).

Other Christians emphasize the second group of passages, those that describe God responding to (rather than controlling) the free actions of human beings. These Christians often have a vibrant sense of God's nearness and His involvement in their lives. They are constantly aware of God's presence in their daily reality. They continually pray because they believe that God hears their prayers and acts according to their desires and requests. But often, in the face of tragedy or adversity, their faith wilts because God seems to have withdrawn His presence all of a sudden. There is no confidence that everything is still going according to plan. They begin to wonder, "Who's in control of the universe anyway?"

Appendix B

This first route is sometimes referred to as "hard" or "high" Calvinism.[17] This view argues that those passages which describe God's changing His mind or responding to the actions of human creatures are just metaphors or figures of speech, sometimes called "anthropomorphic language." That is, God is being described in human terms to accommodate our limited understanding. When Scripture says that God changes His mind, it is no different from those passages that speak of God's having an arm or a hand or eyes. Passages that describe His plan, power, knowledge and sovereignty are taken to be the literal truth. Still, because God is immutable and never changes, these other passages are taken in a figurative sense.

On the other hand, today, there is a movement known as open theism. Open theism in its more extreme forms would have been, undoubtedly, regarded as heretical for most if not all of church history. Unfortunately, today it is making significant inroads into evangelicalism. Open theists teach that God is subject to time, just like we are. He does not control his creation; He can only engage with it. He does not know the future exhaustively, so He can make mistakes. There is an open-ended give and take between God and the world. God is limited in what He can do. He does not know the future exhaustively and cannot control the free decisions of His creatures. Open theists argue that the classical view of a sovereign, all-knowing God is too Greek and philosophical, derived more from Hellenism than from the Scriptures. They argue that God is, in fact, vulnerable. He never interferes with human freedom, so He does not always get His way or accomplish His purposes. God can, and at times must truly, change His mind about things. God is growing through history just as we are. God is in process. He has no plan for the creation, just a wish list.

Now, as the reader can probably tell, neither of these views is congruent with the biblical one. Both have elements of truth, to be sure, but both distort that truth. We must do justice to all that Scripture teaches us about God. It is more important for

---

17 Such readings sometimes are tied to supralapsarian views of decrees.

Christians to submit to the Bible's picture of God than it is for us to understand it. We must simply believe that Scripture teaches us about God without picking and choosing, even if we cannot fit it all together into a neat, coherent package. Otherwise, we make our minds the measure of God's greatness. If we can fully understand God, He isn't God at all.

But, given that there is much mystery here, we still need to pursue this as far as possible. What can we say about these things? How can we move toward glimpsing the full Biblical portrait of who God is? While there is much we cannot fully comprehend, Scripture helps us along the way toward at least some measure of understanding.

In Jonah 3, God sends the prophet to proclaim the message. The message is that in 40 days, Nineveh will be overturned. God is not playing a game with the Ninevites. This prophecy is a real revelation of God's intention toward them at that moment. We know that because after God sees their repentance in verse 10, we are told that God repented. That is to say, God did change His mind. God had announced judgment and the king announced repentance. Therefore, God announced His own repentance. There was a real change in God's relationship with the Ninevites. At point A on the timeline, God intended one thing toward Nineveh; at point B, He intended something else. God said something would happen, then circumstances changed, and what God had declared did not come to pass.

How are we to handle this narrative theologically? Three aspects of Biblical truth can help us here. These are three angles we can take, each of which can enrich our understanding of what is going on in this story. We begin with the simplest to the most complex.

Appendix B

Prophecy

First, we need to understand how prophecy works.[18] There are different kinds of prophecies in Scripture. Some prophecies are simply promises of what God will do. These prophecies are tied to covenant promises and God will perform them, no matter what. We might put in this category prophecies such as the coming of the Messiah, the expansion of the kingdom, and the final judgment. These events are guaranteed; therefore, they cannot not take place. They are not contingent, ultimately, on any human response. They have been revealed as part of God's eternal decree. To make this point, they are often backed up with divine oaths. God swears that He will do these things; or, He says that "my zeal will accomplish these things."

But other prophecies are conditional. Sometimes these conditions are openly stated, and other times they are only implied. These prophecies have to do with God's action within space and time. They are not revelations of the eternal decree per se. Jeremiah 18:1-11 gives us the basic framework for these kinds of divine declarations. In Jeremiah 18, we find that if God intends to bless a nation, and that nation sins and turns away from Him, God will repent and bring judgment against that nation instead of blessing. On the other hand, if God intends harm for a nation and that nation repents, God also will repent, turning from that judgment and giving blessing instead.

---

18 A significant and ground-breaking contribution to this topic came from Dr. Richard Pratt in An Inaugural Address Presented to the Faculty of Reformed Theological Seminary, entitled, "Historical Contingencies and Biblical Predictions." See https://thirdmill.org/newfiles/ric_pratt/TH.Pratt.Historical_Contingencies.html

The principle in Jeremiah 18 applies to all nations. It is not limited to the Jews; it applies to both the Jewish nation and the Gentile nations. It is a principle of how God acts. It is also a principle that helps us to interpret various prophetic passages in Scripture. Consider a few examples. First, take a text that has openly stated conditions. In Isaiah 1, God is speaking to Judah. He says, "If you obey, you will eat the best produce of the land. If you rebel, you will be eaten by the sword." These "if" statements in the prophecy indicate the conditions and the consequences. This prophecy in Isaiah 1 is sort of like a fork in the road, which can go either way, depending on how they respond.

We should understand other prophecies as conditional even though the conditions may not be openly stated. John Calvin said, "Even when the prophets make a simple affirmation, it is to be understood from the outcome that these nonetheless contain a tacit condition."[19] A tacit condition is an unstated but understood condition. For example, in 2 Chronicles 12, a prophet tells Rehoboam that God has left him to be destroyed by Shishak. But Rehoboam repents and the judgment is lessened. There was an implied condition and Rehoboam understood that. In 2 Kings 22, God says to Josiah, "I am bringing disaster to this place." But Josiah repents and the judgment is postponed. There was no condition stated; rather, it was implied. Josiah knew that if he repented, God might do something different. Another example: Hezekiah was told by a prophet in no uncertain terms that Zion would be plowed like a field. The king tore his robes and led his people in repentance, and the judgment was averted. God repented and changed His policy because of their response to the prophecy.

---

19 John Calvin, *Institutes of the Christian Religion*, ed. John T. McNeill, trans. Ford Lewis Battles (Philadelphia, Westminster, 1977), 1.17.14

Appendix B

In each of these cases, God does something other than what He had prophesied because of the human response to His word. Prophecies of this sort do not necessarily reveal to us the divine decree. These are not immutable plans; they reveal God's intentions, apart from intervening historical contingencies.

What kind of prophecy is Jonah 3? It fits the paradigm of Jeremiah 18, obviously. God was going to destroy Nineveh in 40 days if—and here is the implied condition—the people refused to repent. The Ninevite king seemed to understand this. He figured that God could change His mind if the people turned from sin. We know that Jonah understood this principle because we find in chapter 4 that this is what he was afraid of all along. He knew that his message was conditional.

The prophecy in Jonah 3 is not a revelation of God's eternal decree but a conditional declaration of His intentions. It shows us what God intends, but it is also conditional, leaving room for God's intentions to change in time if need be. So one way of dealing with this story, of trying to fit these pieces of the theological jigsaw puzzle together, is to simply acknowledge that God gives the Ninevites a conditional threat that did not necessarily have to happen.

Let us make a quick application here. How are we to read biblical prophecy? Generally, the purpose of prophecy in Scripture is ethical and evangelistic. It is not divine fortune-telling. The purpose of prophecy is to stir us up to repentance and obedience. It is not to satisfy our curiosity about the future. The Ninevites got this point exactly right. They understood that God would typically give a declaration of his intention, watch how the people responded, and then act (or react) accordingly. When we read prophecy in Scripture and seek to apply it, we should never respond with a fatalistic attitude. The purpose of prophecy is ethical, not speculative. So we should always be responding to prophecy with faith and repentance. Prophecy is given to stir us up to produce covenant fidelity, not to satisfy our cravings for knowledge about the future.

Providence

Second, we need to understand God's relationship to the world in all its Biblical complexity. We refer to this as God's providence. As we have seen, God's eternal plan does not and cannot change. However, we must also say that His relationships with His creatures in time can and do change. The universe is not some giant machine. We are not cogs in a cosmic contraption. Reality is not governed by impersonal, natural law. Rather, reality is governed by a personal providence. Indeed, it is governed by the word of God.

God has a plan for the creation, and that plan is the ultimate cause and explanation of everything. But that plan includes the free will choices of men. God brings to pass His plan through the free will decisions that we make (and through other secondary causes). God's immutable plans come to pass in a mysterious way that somehow includes human freedom. How does His plan include human freedom? God does not relate to us the way He relates to rocks or stones. He deals with us, acting in us and upon us, according to our nature as psychologically free, rational, and volitional creatures. Calvin described God's providence this way: "God is watchful, affective, active, engaged in ceaseless activity."[20] Calvin viewed God's providence as a complex interrelationship between God and the world. God is continually acting within His world, ceaselessly active. Calvin said that sometimes God works through an intermediary, sometimes without an intermediary, to accomplish His designs. Calvin balanced his strong affirmation of God's sovereignty with an equally strong commitment to God's complex involvement in creation and responsiveness to His creatures.

---

20 John Calvin, *Institutes of the Christian Religion*, I.16-18

Appendix B

We find the same teaching in the Westminster Confession of Faith. The Westminster Assembly of Divines wrote, "Although in relation to the decree of God, the first cause, all things come to pass immutably and infallibly yet by the same providence He often orders them to fall out according to the nature of secondary causes." The Confession then describes these secondary causes saying that they work together necessarily, freely, or contingently. There is no determinism or fatalism in that! Things happen freely and contingently! The universe is not like a row of dominoes where, when the first one falls, another is sure to fall, and so on. The Confession denies that events are mechanistically determined by what has gone before. The Confession even includes an entire chapter on free will for good measure because the Westminster Assembly of Divines understood that God carries out His fixed plan through the free choices humans make.

God runs the universe, but God works through means (ordinarily). Suppose a tree in the forest gets blown over. Who (or what) caused this? How did this happen? Did God do it or did the wind do it? If we take secondary causes seriously (as we must), our answer will be both. It was God's eternal decree that caused it to happen. But God caused it to occur through the wind that blew through the forest. God is the primary cause; the wind (which God also controls) is the secondary cause.

There is no such thing as natural law in the physical world (e.g., the law of gravity). We can still speak that way, but we need to understand what it means. What we call natural laws are God's ordinary ways of doing things. G. K. Chesterton understood this well. In *Orthodoxy*, he writes, "It's not natural law that makes all daisies the same. It's just that God makes each one individually and he's never gotten tired of making them."[21] It is not natural law that makes natural events recur the same way again and again and again. God's involvement and care are the source of creational consistency.

---

21 G. K. Chesterton, 'The Ethics of Elfland,' in *Orthodoxy* (House of Stratus, 2001), 41.

Thus, we should never speak of God intervening or interfering with things in the world. If we live and move and have our being in God, then God is never on the outside needing to break into our world. He is always already active and working. God is no more active or at work in the miraculous than He is in the non-miraculous. The ordinary and the extraordinary are both God's doing. Therefore, God is never an intruder in His universe.

So, with this understanding of God's complex relationship to the world, it should not surprise us at all that God responded to the Ninevites as He did. God is always involved in everything, and under His sovereignty our choices and actions shape the course and direction of history. They are a part of God's plan. But understand that God's plan does not make our repentance and our prayers and our obedience unnecessary. It is just the opposite. It is precisely that plan that gives these human actions their meaning and their efficacy. Therefore, secondary causes are real and effectual.

Personality

Finally, we need to develop a deeper understanding of prophecy, providence, and God's personality. As we saw earlier, He is the author of the story of history. But more than that, He also is a character within the story. He has written himself into the script, so He responds and engages. He acts dynamically and relationally within the creation and within time. He is a God who is far away but also, as Jeremiah says, a God who is near. He is transcendent, but He is also immanent. He is, to put it simply, the living God. He is not the watchmaker in the sky who wound up the world to run on its own. He is personally active in His creation, acting and reacting at all times. He initiates and He responds.

There is fierceness and freedom in God's action. Like C. S. Lewis's Aslan, God is good, but He is not tame. There is a perfect wisdom to His ways, a perfect logic even. But at the same time, He is totally unpredictable and incomprehensible. He astonishes us

Appendix B

with the unexpected. He loves plot twists and surprise endings. Just look at the story in Jonah. It is full of surprises. Why Nineveh, after all? What a shock—that God would elect these pagan barbarians for salvation! Why Jonah? This is a surprise as well. Why this obstinate, hard-headed prophet? Why not somebody else more obedient and "with it"? And why did God change His mind? Why announce destruction, only to turn away from it? This is another surprising twist to the story.

In C.S. Lewis' series, *The Chronicles of Narnia*, Lucy spies on Aslan over a ridge. Lucy notes to herself that Aslan looks different than when she had seen him before. She runs up to him and says, "Aslan! You're so much bigger!" He growls at her out of affection, and says, "No, little child. I am no bigger. But every time you grow, I will look bigger to you."[22]

As we come to know God more and more, we find His mysteriousness increasing rather than decreasing. We know more of Him, but our deeper and more intimate knowledge only reveals how much of Him we still cannot grasp. Our God, like Aslan, is a God on the move. He is a God who will only be pinned down one place—the cross (the stone table in Lewis' story)—and even then, it is only a matter of three days and nights before he is on the loose again. Once more, as Lewis describes Aslan, so it is with the biblical God: He is good, but not safe. He is not the god of the philosophers; He is the God of the storytellers. He is not a being whose existence can be reduced to a set of propositions or concepts; He is too full of life and vigor and vitality for that kind of dissection-like analysis.

We have to guard ourselves against de-personalizing God. God is not the Unmoved Mover or the First Cause or the Ground of All Being. These are common philosophical descriptions of God, and no doubt they have a grain of truth. But, taken by themselves,

---

22 C.S. Lewis, *Prince Caspian: The Return to Narnia,* The Chronicles of Narnia (New York: HarperCollins Publishers, 1994), 141.

they suck the life, the personality, and the freedom out of God. God is the Creator of all human personality, which is designed to reflect his own personal existence.

In the Bible's stories and poetry, God is jealous and He expresses joy and delight. He says He feels grief and pain, love and hate. He shows patience, and He shows wrath. And yes, he even repents. He is not a detached or disinterested, or uninvolved God. He is a God who sends shipwrecking storms to recover runaway prophets. He is a God who sends great fish to do His bidding. He is a God who gives second chances, who has compassion on livestock, and who sends hot winds to irritate His own prophets. He is a God whose heart is, as Judges 9 says, gladdened by wine. He is the God who raises up the lowly and brings down the mighty. He is the God who feels the pain of His people. He is the God who puts on human flesh and lays down His life to secure the salvation of His bride.

The God of the book of Jonah will not be put in a box. Jonah wanted to stuff God into a box, but Jonah found that God is the God who breaks boxes. He defies our attempts to pin Him down like a frog in freshman biology class. This is the Biblical picture of who God is—or perhaps we should say it is the motion picture of who God is because He does not sit still long enough for us to paint His portrait. He is always on the move and cannot be domesticated. He is the living God, full of vigor, action, and passion. We cannot confine Him or contain Him. We cannot exhaust Him in a book of theological propositions nor squeeze Him into the smallness of our private religious experiences.

Does God Change His Mind?

So, finally, let us return to the question we began with: what exactly does Jonah 3:10 mean? How do we tie together God's sovereignty and responsiveness? His transcendence with His immanence? Does God change His mind? No. God does not change His mind. He does not change His mind if by that we mean that God's eternal decree can change or that God can be misinformed or surprised or mistaken. God is not dependent on His creation in any way. And if God had to change His mind, that would be bad news for us because it would mean God is limited just like we are. If God has no control over history, if He does not know what the future holds, then all hope is lost. Chaos would be king, and the world would be adrift at sea without a rudder or an anchor. So no, God cannot change His mind. He is utterly sovereign and His eternal plan determines whatsoever comes to pass.

But, on the other hand, God can and does change His mind in the sense that He is involved, responsive, and engaging. God not only stands outside creation as the sovereign and transcendent ruler of the universe. He also inhabits His creation, acting and reacting within it in various complex and personal ways. He is in personal relationship with us, a changing relationship in which He responds to us and we respond to Him.

God is not only transcendent, existing outside of time and space; He also is immanent, filling time and space. Our free choices are part of His plan, and so, in some mysterious way, they shape (in a secondary way) the course that history takes. He has planned our course, but He also reacts to each step we take. Through our actions, we can please God or grieve Him. We can pray for blessing and receive it or miss out on a blessing because of prayerlessness. God plans our prayers but also acts to answer prayer. Certain things will happen or will not happen depending on whether or not we pray. God not only acts, He also reacts. He not only plans, but He also responds.

So, does God change his mind? Yes. We had better hope that God changes His mind because this is our only hope. It is what makes the salvation of sinners possible. The Ninevites knew that God's changing His mind and relenting was their only hope. And because they understood this, Nineveh repented and received a reprieve. God changed His mind about them, turning wrath into grace.

The good news is that God has changed His mind about us as well. By nature, we are in Adam under God's wrath because of the sin of our first parents. Like Nineveh, we stand under a threat of judgment. But God changed His mind about you at the cross. God relented, in principle, when Jesus' blood made propitiation. That change of mind became a fact when the Spirit drew us to Christ in faith and repentance.

While we were still His enemies, Christ died for us so that God might befriend us once again. At the cross, God relented from wrath. At Calvary, God repented of the great evil that He had in store for us. He changed His mind about us.

God's "repentance" in Christ is the source of our hope and salvation. The cross of Christ reveals God's desire to save sinners, to turn every act of wrath into an act of grace. At Noah's flood, God grieves that He made man, but at the cross, God rejoices in man once again, for now sin has been paid for and enmity has been transformed into friendship. Now we can feel the warmth of God's smile and love upon us once again. In 1 Samuel 15, God grieves that He made Saul king. But now He rejoices in having made Jesus King and in seating us with Him in heavenly places. God's anger has been exhausted in Christ. God now offers us a peace treaty.

Appendix C

Singing Zion's Songs in a Foreign Land:

Jonah and the Missional Church

Jonah 1:17-2:10 and Psalm 137

The Story of Exile and Exodus

We live in a post-Christian, biblically illiterate society. Bible stories that once defined and shaped our culture have long since been forgotten. There is a decent chance that your non-Christian neighbor, even in the so-called Bible Belt, does not know the name of Adam's wife, or who built the ark, or who denied Jesus three times. In the church, things are a little better. We still know the stories, usually, but we tend to know them in bits and pieces. We tend to know them in a fragmented way. We know them in isolation but not in their broader context, as wholes. We may know the story of Abraham and the story of Joseph and the story of Moses and the story of Jonah and the story of Jesus, but we do not know how they all fit together as one story. We do not see how they all connect. Instead, we treat them as free-floating, independent units rather than integrating them into a single Biblical narrative that runs from Genesis to Revelation. Thus, we tend to think that we outgrow these stories with age. We think these stories are great for children, for Sunday School, and Vacation Bible School, but when we grow up, we can forget the stories and just focus on Paul. We think that we graduate from the Old Testament narratives to Pauline theology. The Reformed tradition tends to read and write book after book after book on systematic theology or Romans and Galatians. Therefore, we neglect the Old Testament stories.

In reality, we never outgrow Bible stories. Every culture is defined by its stories. Ancient Greece was defined by the stories of Homer and Hesiod. Ancient Rome was defined by the story of Romulus and Remus. The modern West is defined by the stories of Darwin and Rousseau. But the church's culture is defined by the Bible's story. It is this story that gives us our identity; it is this story that gives us a focused lens through which we can view ourselves, the world, and the rest of history outside the Bible.

Throughout Scripture, we find the entire story of the Bible summarized for us in miniature form. We have these little microcosms that give us the big picture, putting the whole story in bite-size. Most frequently, the story of the Bible is summed up as the story of death and resurrection, or as the story of exile and exodus. Consider some ways that these plot-lines define the entire story of the Bible.

The Adamic Story

At the beginning of the Bible's story, Adam sins, and so he dies. From dust he came and to dust he will return. But through a second Adam who undergoes the penalty of death, though He is sinless, God accomplishes resurrection. God restores what was lost in the first Adam and even glorifies it. The resurrection does not simply take us back to square one, back to Adam in the Garden; rather, it gives us a quantum leap forward from childhood to maturity, from initial glory to final glory. Adam had dominion over the earth, but Jesus said all authority, not only on earth but also in heaven, has been made His possession. Adam had an earthly glory, but Jesus has heavenly glory. Adam had God's favor but could lose it. For Jesus, there is no such possibility. Jesus' resurrection was a representative event. Already He has brought us, as His people, into this new life of the resurrection. We share in His resurrection glory and reign and even in His heavenly life even now. And we know that since His story had a happy ending that our story will also. His story, in effect, has become our story. We are assured of our future bodily resurrection and our future glory. In a nutshell, that is the Bible's story: Death in Adam and resurrection in Jesus Christ as the last Adam.

There are several stories in scripture that encapsulate this whole death and resurrection theme. For example, consider the so-called "binding of Isaac" story in Genesis 22. Abraham is willing to offer his son Isaac sacrificially. Thus, he receives him back from the dead, figuratively speaking (as the writer of Hebrews says). As a result, Isaac undergoes a form of death and resurrection. In the story, Abraham plays the role of God the Father. Isaac is cast in the role of God the Son. Together, they act out symbolically what the Father and the Son do in reality in the gospels. It is the whole Bible in one chapter.

Another way to look at the Biblical story as a whole is through the categories of exile and exodus. When Adam sins, he is exiled from the Garden of Eden. We see his banishment in that God stations cherubim with flaming swords to guard the way back into Eden. Adam is not allowed back into the garden sanctuary. The rest of scripture, then, is simply about exodus. It is about being brought back into God's presence, being freed from bondage to the world, to the flesh, and the devil, so that we can come, once again, into the Promised Land of God's sanctuary. The whole Tabernacle and Temple systems showed that access had not yet been granted to the people under the Old Covenant. They had veils that kept the people out of the innermost sanctuary where God was present to show the people that they were still in Adam, and therefore still in exile. When Jesus died, of course, that veil was torn from top to bottom. When Jesus ascended up into heaven, He took His people with him (Eph. 4:8; cf. Eph. 2:6; Col. 3:1ff). He restored their access to the heavenly sanctuary. In Luke 9:31, Jesus even refers to His death as an exodus. He is going to bring the exile to an end at His cross and restore us to the presence of God. He regains for us the access to God that Adam lost. We were exiled in Adam; we are exodused in Christ. Again, that, in a nutshell, is the story of the Bible.

The Church in Exile

Jonah is one of those smaller stories that sums up the big story that the entire Bible tells. Jonah undergoes death and resurrection when swallowed by the great creature and then spit back out onto dry land. That is how his prayer describes the whole event in Jonah 2—as a trip to Sheol and back.

But he also undergoes an exile and return. He is cast away from God's presence (2:3-4) and then restored (2:7-9). In this way, Jonah gives Israel a symbolic prophecy of what her history will look like in the short run and what the church's history will look like in the long run. This section aims to look at Jonah as a story of exile and exodus and then make some applications to the church today. If this is our defining story, the story that gives us our identity and shapes our vocation, we should be able to use it as a lens for interpreting our current situation as Christians living in 21st century America.

The Symbols in Jonah

We can better handle how this works if we look at some of the basic symbols that show up in the Jonah narrative. In the Bible's worldview, everything that God made is symbolic.[23] God designed the world as a system of symbols through which He

---

23 For a superb introduction to symbolism, see, James B. Jordan, *Through New Eyes: Developing a Biblical View of the World* (Eugene, Oregon: Wipf and Stock Publishers, 1999).

reveals himself and His purposes. As modern people, we tend to look at the world in scientific terms rather than symbolic terms. We look at the stars and think in terms of physics, seeing only flaming balls of gas. We look at an animal and think in terms of biology rather than the symbolic significance of that animal. This scientific way of looking at the world is good and necessary. But it does not go far enough. The Bible describes the world in terms of symbolic images, just as it describes history in terms of repeating patterns (typology). Both creation and the history that takes place within the created order are designed by God, and God has filled everything with beauty, order, meaning, and significance. Jonah's view of the world is shaped by the rest of Scripture. Thus, when Jonah speaks of the sea, we should not just think of water. The sea, especially the roaring, foaming, stormy sea, appears throughout scripture as a picture of the Gentile nation's rebellion against God. In Psalm 65:7, the noise of the waves is parallel to the tumult of the nations. In Isaiah 17:12, the nations are compared to the roar of the sea. In Isaiah 5:30, Assyria is depicted as the wild, chaotic sea.

In the biblical imagery, the sea is always trying to overcome the land. Picture it: if we are on the beach, the waves roll up, and it looks like they are going to try to gobble up the land and overcome it. But then they roll back down, and the land re-emerges. This points to another set of passages in the Old Testament—those that speak of God restraining the sea and holding the waters within their proper bounds (cf. Gen. 1:6-10; Job 38:8-11). This is a picture of God's holding the Gentile nations in their place. He will not allow them to overcome the land, which is symbolic (as we will see just below) of Israel.

The great fish is also a Gentile symbol. In Psalm 74, the great sea monster is used as a picture of Egypt. In Jeremiah 51, Babylon is a great sea monster that swallows up Judah (southern Israel) and then spits him out. This is a picture of exile and exodus. Thus, the fish in the story of Jonah must symbolize a Gentile empire. Sea and fish together give this book a Gentile flavoring.

Meanwhile, land imagery in this book and throughout Scripture is associated with Israel. In Genesis 12, God promises Abraham a special land. Israel rules over the land as a new Adam. God binds Abraham's family to the earth. When Israel sins, the basic curse of the covenant is that she loses the land. When scripture speaks of God as ruler over land and sea (cf. Jonah 1:9), we could read that as saying that God is the God of both Jew and Gentile. Israel is like an island of covenant fidelity amongst the sea of pagan Gentiles. When God keeps the sea at bay, restraining the waves, it is a picture of His protecting Israel (the land) against the Gentile nations. But when God lets those restraints go, the water begins to surround and wash over Israel. This symbolizes Israel's being overwhelmed and conquered. Jonah describes this precisely in Jonah 2:3, 5-6.

We can explore this symbolic matrix further. After God calls Abraham, everything in the Old Testament is land-oriented. God chooses land workers, mainly farmers and shepherds, to do his work (e.g., David, Amos). All the action takes place on land. There is one exception—the book of Jonah. Jonah deals with the sea, with sailors, with a boat, with a fish, and with sea travel. Of course, this is because it deals with a mission to the Gentiles. The book of Jonah is a sign of things to come. It deals with ministering to the nations outside the land of promise. It is relatively unique in the Old Testament in this way, but it is a pointer to the new covenant situation.

In the gospels, we find that Jesus calls several fishermen rather than farmers or shepherds to be His disciples. He says that they will be fishers of men. That is, they will preach to Gentiles, "hooking" them with the Gospel. During His ministry, Jesus is always around water, crossing the sea, or feeding people fish, or eating fish Himself, or walking on water, or calming the sea. All of these things are symbolic. Through Jesus, the Gospel will go out to the sea/nations.

The rest of New Testament fleshes out this shift. In the book of Acts, we find Paul carrying the Gospel abroad over the sea in a boat, moving from Jerusalem to the nations. All of this water activity in the New Testament symbolizes the Gospel in its fullness going forth to the Gentiles. Also relevant is the symbolic picture in Revelation 10 of Jesus, the Son of man, taking an oath, as He has one foot on the land and one foot in the water. It is a picture of Jesus' uniting both Jew and Gentile (land and sea) into this one new covenant community (cf. Eph. 2:11ff).

With this kind of biblical background, it is easy to see what is going on in Jonah. It is not a stretch at all to see this symbolism at work. Jonah is cast into the sea, which means that Israel is going to be cast into exile. She is going to be taken out of her land and thrown into the raging sea of the Gentile nations. However, just as with Jonah, the Lord is preparing a great fish for her. The Assyrian empire will swallow Israel whole. In Assyria, Israel will be afflicted and distressed, but she will survive. The Lord's preservation of Jonah in the fish is a frightening promise. Still, it is a promise that Israel will be protected for a symbolic period of three days and three nights in the belly of Assyria. God will take care of Israel through the exilic period. And just as Jonah has his exodus and returns to dry land, so in due time the pagan powers will send Israel back to her land and she will be restored in her prophetic calling. She will be vomited back onto the land in a new exodus. Jonah's experience is prophetic: Israel will undergo a death and resurrection just as Jonah did, an exile and exodus even as Jonah did.[24]

Typology, History, and Opportunity

Because typology is not well understood in the church today, we need to dwell a little more on how this reading of Jonah works. Typology is different from allegory. Sometimes we will hear that the Reformation broke with the medieval way of allegorizing Scripture, and to a large extent, that is true. But the Reformers did not give up on typology. Thus, we need to distinguish between

---

24 The same thing is going to happen to Judah (southern Israel) a bit later in history. The prophet Jeremiah speaks of Judah being swallowed up by the Babylonian empire for 70 years and then being spit back out into her land.

allegory and typology. Allegory turns historical narratives into philosophical ideas or into abstract concepts. Typology, by contrast, is rooted in history. Typology looks for God's impression, or stamp, on historical events. It looks for God's design in the music and rhythm of history. And once the basic pattern has been discerned, we know what to do with that passage of Scripture. We can look for the same kind of patterns in church history outside of the Bible. The patterns in scripture give us a model for understanding and grappling with our own situations. When we get in tune with God's rhythms in history, we see (at least to some extent) where history is moving, and we can begin to see how we ought to respond. We can begin to prepare for what God is going to do next. We reason by analogy from biblical history to our own situation. We look for various links and connections, so we make concrete applications.

When we begin to embrace how God carries history along with the patterns that He has impressed into historical sequences, we can begin to decode our own situation. We can begin to interpret our own situation and use the Scriptures to guide our response. We can understand the times and know what the new Israel ought to do (2 Chron. 12:32). We can begin to prepare for the future, using the Scriptures as our compass to chart our course and set our agenda.[25]

The American Church is in an exilic situation today. Like Jonah/Israel, we fell asleep on the job, compromising our calling to be a prophetic light to the world around us. For many centuries the church had the upper hand in Western culture and particularly in our American culture. America was, at least plausibly, a Christian nation. We demonstrated in many ways a Christian work ethic and upheld in many ways Christian moral standards. These things were imperfectly predominant in our national culture, but they were respected and valued in our nation. We were continuing in

---

[25] James B. Jordan, *Crisis, Opportunity, and the Christian Future* (West Monroe, Louisiana: Athanasius Press, 1994; repr. 2016). We draw heavily on Jordan's book here.

the tradition of Christendom. The state (the political order) was at least attentive to the church somehow, if not openly supportive of her. As recently as 1892, the Supreme Court declared that America is publicly a Christian nation. As recently as 1947, the President could emphatically declare that America is a Christian, Protestant nation.

But now, on our watch, America has rejected that heritage. The heritage of Christendom stretches back, not just to the founding fathers or to the colonial Puritans or to the Reformers, but back to Charlemagne, Augustine and Constantine. But we have made a quite decisive, and even self-conscious, break with the historic Christian faith and the Christendom that built Western civilization. We have returned to something of a pre-Constantinian situation. And so, American Christians, without being driven from our homeland geographically, have entered into something of an exile situation. She is exiled from a place of cultural influence, social respect, and a place of political centrality. Christendom, in other words, is over. We are aliens and strangers in a deeper way than we have been for quite some time.

People in our culture spends billions and billions of dollars each year on entertainment that cultivates nothing but hatred for God. Christian symbols and stories have been systematically eliminated from public life, buildings, education, and the arts. It has become impossible to appeal to the Bible in the public forum or in public debate because the Bible is considered a sectarian book. It is not a religiously neutral standard; therefore, it cannot be used. It does not pass the tests of reason and science and so it is ruled out of court. The Bible has been privatized, viewed as nothing more than a handbook for individualistic spirituality.

Christians disagree on how to cope with the end of Christendom. Most, of course, see it as a bad thing and it is a bad thing, but it can also be a good thing for us. That is the paradox of exile: it is both blessing and curse. Tragically, we have legalized abortion in our country and desensitized ourselves to blasphemy and violence. All of these things are signs of God's disciplinary hand resting upon us. But the end of Christian civilization in the

West also offers us unparalleled opportunities, just as the exile did for Israel. For Israel, the exile ended up spreading the true faith across the known world, something that never would have happened otherwise.

For us, the end of Christendom means that we have great opportunities as well. There were a lot of problems in the old form of Christendom, like self-righteousness and complacency. The church now has a chance to humble herself, to present a different sort of public face to a watching world. She has the opportunity to learn better how to serve, love, forgive—all, of course, with the hope of building a better and stronger foundation for a future Christendom. God never stops at death, which means that the story never ends with exile. He always brings about a resurrection and an exodus. So, while we live in a post-Christian culture, there is also a sense in which we live in a pre-Christian culture. God is not going to leave His church in the belly of an apostate empire forever.

The question, though, is what do we do in the meantime? What matters most is not reminiscing about "the good ol' days" or wishing we lived in a different era. Instead, what matters most is figuring out how to articulate and adorn the Gospel in our time and place. This is our time on the center stage of redemptive history, and we need to make the most of it.

How do we, as Christians, learn to live as strangers and aliens in our country? What is the church supposed to be doing? If we are in an exile chapter in the church's story, waiting to enter into a new exodus chapter, what should our agenda be in the meantime? What should drive us? What map should guide us? What kinds of things should we be looking to do?[26]

---

[26] While the church may be entering into exile in the West, in other parts of the world, she is in full conquest mode. We need to avoid any kind of Western-centrism that measures everything by our own civilization's status. See Phillip Jenkins' book, *The Next Christendom: The Coming of Global Christianity*, for a look at the church's explosive growth in other parts of the globe.

A crucial text in our orientation toward our present time is the exilic Psalm 137, written by and for Jewish exiles living in Babylon. The exiles weep as they think back on life in the Promised Land (their version of Christendom—"the good ol' days"). It was a glorious and wonderful thing and they are sad to have left it. One of their captors asks, almost tormenting them, "Will you sing us one of Zion's songs?" (137:3). The Israelite reply is, "How shall we sing the Lord's song in a foreign land?" (137:4). That is, "How can we sing Zion's songs in exile? How can we rejoice outside the Promised Land? How can we sing the songs of the kingdom when the kingdom is in eclipse?"

Jonah 2 answers that question posed in Psalm 137, but it phrases the question a bit differently. Jonah spins the question this way: Can Jonah sing Zion's songs from the belly of the fish? Answering that question will answer the question, "Can Israel sing Zion's songs in exile? Can she sing Zion's songs in the belly of the fish that is Assyria?" The answer we get back from the book of Jonah is a resounding yes! If we do not sing Zion's songs that reflect God's joy and God's glory, we will be just like Jonah at the beginning and end of the book, rather than like Jonah in the middle of the book.

As Christians get more and more pushed out to the margins of our culture, the temptation is for us to batten down the hatches and become more and more narrow-minded and narrow-hearted. The temptation is to settle for simply being a subculture rather than a counterculture. The temptation for Christian exiles is to adopt an "us-versus-them" posture so that we antagonize the world rather than serve the world. Unfortunately, such an approach only drives us that much deeper into exile.[27]

It is simply not enough to say to apostate American culture, "We're right and you're wrong on moral issues." That is true, and those things must be said. But that alone is not an adequate

---

27 This is not to deny that the church is at war. She must stand against the world, but the way we wage holy war in the New Covenant is through sacrifice and service, preaching and praise.

response on the part of the church. Such pronouncements on their own look arrogant to an unbelieving culture and will not fix anything. Jesus could have said in a detached way, "My way of being Israel is right and yours is wrong." But that is not what He did. In Matthew 23, we find Jesus weeping over His unbelieving countrymen. Paul does the same in Romans 9, where he laments the infidelity of the apostate Jews. Jesus and Paul were filled with compassion toward the lost.

An Agenda for Exile

How does this shape our understanding of the church's agenda for today? America is not Israel. But there is an analogy. We need to ask: How do we view our fellow Americans who do not believe the Gospel? Do we weep over them, or do we boast over them? Do we despise them, or do we show them holy compassion? These are the kinds of questions we must ask.

When Jesus said in the Sermon on the Mount in Matthew 5, "Love your enemies," He is speaking to an Israel that is still in exile. Even though Israel had returned to her land many centuries before, she still understood herself in exile because she was still under pagan domination (Ezra 9:9; Dan. 9). She had returned from exile geographically, but at a deeper level, she was still exiled. So, when Jesus says, "Love your enemies," it is evident which enemies He has in view. He is talking about how to deal with the Romans, Israel's wicked oppressors. So the question Jesus asks is, "What are the Israelites to do as a people in exile under Roman oppression, under a regime that hates the true God?"

Jesus says the same thing Jeremiah said, as Israel was going to be carted off into exile. Jeremiah told the people, "Seek the good of the city where you're being taken. Seeks its peace and prosperity" (cf. Jer. 29). Jesus is saying the same thing in different languages, extending Jeremiah's program down to His day. When the covenant people are exiled, they continue to live as God's distinct people, but they cannot check out on society and enter into a covenant ghetto.

For Jonah, this calling meant preaching, teaching, and discipling the Ninevites. Jonah needed to learn about the breadth and scope of God's redemptive purposes in the world. He needed to share in God's mission to the lost.

Similarly, we must figure out what this means for us. It does not mean minimizing God's holy hatred for what American culture has become. Our culture's greed, lust, laziness, violence, and so on must be challenged directly with the Gospel. But it also means we must not forget the love and compassion of God even toward the wicked. It means that we cannot simply seek our own good instead of the city's good or the nation's good. Simply put, being right is not enough.

If Zion's songs come to mold us and shape us and form us, we can hold two things together that the rest of American culture cannot.[28] We can hold together holiness and compassion. Without the songs of Zion on our lips, we can be either ethical or merciful, but never both. Thus, we end up with twisted counterfeits of the biblical virtues.

There are two extreme ways of looking at the American situation that people in our culture gravitate toward, not just in the culture at large but also in the church. There are "conservatives" who focus on individual ethics, and there are "liberals" who focus on corporate compassion. As we profile these opposite positions, it becomes evident they are distortions of the biblical view. Thus, there is a deep and pressing need for the church to spell out a tertium quid (a third way).

By the ethical person here, we speak of the person who thinks that everyone should get what they deserve. It is the person who says, "I pulled myself up by my own bootstraps, so others should be able to do the same. I don't care what their situation is." This

---

[28] Zion's songs are psalmically shaped, including the psalms themselves and worship songs that reflect the joyful reverence of the Gospel.

person forgets how much they have that they did not earn. This person comes off looking holier-than-thou in his attitude. This mindset prevails among a lot of American conservatives.

What will the songs of Zion do to this kind person? As we sing these songs of death and resurrection, they will humble this kind of person. They will eradicate any sense he has of being a self-made man because these songs will proclaim that salvation is of the Lord. The songs of Zion will teach that person that while he should hold himself to a high standard because God does, he should be humble and patient toward others because God Himself is humble and patient.

On the other hand, there is the kind of person who emphasizes compassion. But because this compassion is divorced from holiness rather than mixed with it, the compassion is distorted. So he ends up relativizing everything, and ethics do not matter so long as nobody gets hurt.

What will the songs of Zion do in this case? These songs will remind this person that while God is compassionate, his compassion comes with conditions. There must be repentance, faithfulness, obedience, and holiness. Compassion may be "free grace," but it is not "cheap grace."[29]

It is only as these songs of Zion form and fashion us that we can hold these things together and become a truly countercultural people, rather than sub-cultural or anti-cultural. Songs like Jonah's psalm and Psalm 137 will create in us the right blend of holy boldness and sacrificial love. In the midst of an exilic situation, we face all kinds of challenges. We must live out our faith in the public square, but in a way that manifests charity and humility. We must strive to combine holiness with compassion, discipline with mercy, and obedience with grace.

The church offers a third way to minister effectively in our culture. We offer an alternative to the standard categories of American politics, a counter-politics that takes both individual

---

[29] See Dietrich Bonhoeffer's *The Cost of Discipleship* for a development of this theme of cheap grace.

responsibility and corporate compassion seriously, emphasizing both righteousness and kindness. When we hold these things together, we become effective in seeking to transform and reclaim our culture. We must remember: the point is not to win a debate or argument but to persuade people to embrace Christ as King.

People in exile are at their best when they are humble about their distinctives. If we do not balance holiness and compassion, we look like arrogant conservatives or bleeding-heart liberals. Our solutions to culture's problems, then, become indistinguishable from other Americans. We become assimilated into the pre-existing American political climate.

Conservatism can fall into this trap. When it comes to offering solutions, they simply blend in with a conservative status quo. In other branches of the church, they blend in with the liberal status quo. The church must recover a sense of being sent into the world as the bearer of both God's grace and holiness, even as Jonah was sent to Ninevah as the bearer of God's message.

It was this mission that Israel refused to carry out on behalf of the nations. God sent Israel to the nations to teach them, but she refused to go, even as Jonah refused to go. Thus, God sent Israel to the nations in another way—through exile. But the exile served God's purpose, for in exile, Israel began to fulfill her missional vocation of bearing witness to the nations as God had called her to do.

Putting the Exilic Agenda Into Practice

How do we go about this? How do we live distinctively without self-righteousness? How do we show compassion without moral laxity? How do we make the Gospel attractive in a culture that hates the living God?

First, we have got to find ways to show that the Bible is a public book. We must find ways to show that the Bible answers the deepest "spiritual" questions that individuals can ask and the most important political questions that a society can ask. The answers the Bible gives are sound, true, and workable.

We must proclaim to our communities that God is at work in the world today. In particular, we must teach and show people that God is active in and through the church. Even though His prophets may sleep from time to time (like Jonah), God never sleeps or slumbers. God is always at work and always available to those who call upon Him. Finally, we have to teach people that God answers prayer offered up to Him in His true temple, the Church of Jesus Christ.

We need to learn that the church is our true homeland. We need to tell new converts, "You're not from America anymore. You're from the Jerusalem that is above. She is your mother city." This does not obliterate all loyalties to earthly regimes, but it does relativize those loyalties. The Nicene Creed trumps the Pledge of Allegiance. The cross must be put above the flag. The church's courts are the first place to look for the settling of civil disputes.

We have to do the work of discipleship so that Americans come to know that salvation is of the Lord, and that those who cling to worthless American idols, like money and pleasure, are forfeiting their only opportunity for mercy. We have to teach America that Jesus is King and that the church is His empire—indeed, the church is the only lasting and international world empire there is. Other empires will come and go but the church lasts forever. As Theodore Beza said, "The church is an anvil that has worn out many a hammer." We need to teach America that even the most powerful politicians are, as Augustine said, "bound to make their power the handmaid of God's majesty."

Most of all, we have to call America to join with us in giving sacrificial worship to the God of all creation. Only when God is loved as He ought to be loved can there be true love offered toward others. In his work, *The City of God*, Augustine said that any true commonwealth, any true social order, must be based on justice.

Augustine had a quite Hebraic, covenantal understanding of justice in view. Augustine said that justice is based on giving each his due, which begins with giving God His due. In other words, Augustine is saying that worship is central to everything, even to politics. Worshipping God is the master key to a just society. A true social order is based on the Eucharist, where we give thanks to God through the body and blood of His Son and feast together as a community of diverse but united persons.

This is our task as exiles: To live these things out, revealing and embodying these truths in our community. This is not simply a matter of our words but also of our deeds. It is not enough to have these truths on our lips; we must enact them in our lives as well. We might even say that this is the core of Christian political practice. Remember, fundamentally, "politics" has to do with how we structure our life together in the polis (the city). In the church, we must show forth the true sacrificial politics—a Gospel-based, Eucharistic politics. The church must show that she is God's true family and city, the place where we find genuine community. By her common life, she must show what true humanity looks like, what God intended for human life to be and do. In this way, the church becomes a model for the rest of society.

We may be a remnant, exilic community, but as we sing and live by Zion's songs, even in a foreign land like America, we will find things beginning to change. We will find the world around us beginning to be transformed, bit by bit. As we seek the good of the city, as we carry out our mission to disciple this culture in terms of God's holiness and compassion, we will find God's resurrecting power at work. We may find life in the belly of the fish more bearable (for as long as it lasts) if songs like Jonah's are filling our hearts. And we may even find ourselves spit back out onto dry land sooner than we would have thought. Let us pray that God would make this so.

www.ingramcontent.com/pod-product-compliance
Lightning Source LLC
Chambersburg PA
CBHW071855070526
44583CB00016B/1699